SHINE ON YOU CRAZY DAISY
- VOLUME 5

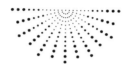

COMPILED BY TRUDY SIMMONS

CONTENTS

Printed in the United Kingdom
First Printing, April 2022

ISBN: 9781739914882 (paperback)
ISBN: 9781739914899 (eBook)

The Daisy Chain Group International Ltd
Hampshire, UK
connect@thedaisychaingroup.com

This book is dedicated to....
....All the businesswomen that are showing up and putting themselves out there to be seen and heard. We are all in this together... this is for you to take inspiration, that we are all on a similar journey, but taking different paths, with varying bumps along the way to here.
You can do it! Keep going!
Shine Bright and Shine On.

ACKNOWLEDGMENTS

This is to acknowledge and appreciate all of those that have contributed and shared a piece of their journey with us all in this book. Thank you for your courage and tenacity. You are all inspirational.

As you will read in this book, success is different for everyone. The way that we decide what success means to us, and how we get there, is a culmination of 1000s of choices and decisions that we make in our businesses.

Here is to the lessons we didn't want to learn; that we didn't know we had to learn to get us to where we are now. Be grateful for the good AND the bad.

Each of these brilliant businesswomen have shared a part of their journey and each of us knows, that we can't do it alone, we aren't meant to do it alone. Surround yourself with the people that "get it".

To the Facebook communities that I run – Businesswomen Shine Online and Hampshire Women's Business Group for showing me each and every day that whatever we are going through, we are all there for each other. For being the communities that we all call "our lounge-room" where we come to share, ask for help, support, advice and give from our expertise without expectations. I am grateful for the "tribe" that we have and that like attracts like. Community is everything on this lonely road. Come and join ours, it is the best – tee hee!

I stand for inclusion on all aspects. The baseline of everything that we build is on kindness and being available with open arms to all businesswomen that wish to be a part of something and want to be seen and heard. We are here for all of that.

Welcome.

INTRODUCTION

This book is about creating a platform for businesswomen to have an inspirational voice and to share their stories with others, to show that this entrepreneurial rollercoaster is the highs AND the lows and that we navigate them all differently, but hopefully with a tribe/team of people that support our vision to our success – whatever that looks like, and it is different for everyone.

Each story is unique, each story is REAL, each story offers a piece of insight, motivation and encouragement when we need it the most. You are not alone.

These are un-edited chapters of real stories from women that have been where you are and have stories to share about how to find your way, not feel isolated, find out what you CAN do, rather than feeling stuck in what you think you can't do.

Here…. Are their stories!! Bong bong…

Charity donation

As we gain, so can we give – that is my philosophy of running my own business. 10% of the profits from this book will be donated to the bereaved families of the NHS who have died while looking after us and our families during the Corona-Virus pandemic.

To find out more, or to donate, please visit this website

www.healthcareworkersfoundation.org

COMMIT TO YOURSELF

Trudy Simmons

Are you sitting comfortably? Then let's begin…

A lot of our stories start with how our commitment to "something" has changed. We were committed to a job, then we lost that commitment and changed. We have had children, and our priorities and commitments change. We find partners, and our commitments change.

Everything starts with a renewed commitment to that thing and a letting go of what we thought was a commitment before. That is our how stories change, progress, and grow…

And guess what… it's the same in business.

Recently, I created a challenge in our Shine On You Crazy Daisy VIP Membership to commit to ourselves in whatever way suited each person for 1 month. Easy peasy lemon squeezy, right? But everyone has all the "other things" going on in our lives, so the LAST thing we do is find the time, energy, head space, and COMMITMENT to give to ourselves. So we switched up the thinking and committed to each other that we would do:

· 10 pages of reading a day
· A yoga session
· A 2 mile walk
· Exercise for 30 mins 3 times a week
· Meditate for 20 mins
· An afternoon nap of 20 mins

We picked 2 of those things to do each day, and we chose which they were, on a daily basis. Most importantly, we committed to EACH OTHER that it would be done. We became women of science, a social experiment to see what would happen.

Now the brilliance of the VIP membership is that it is all about accountability for your business. Say what you want to be held accountable to, and then COMMIT to getting it done. So the concept of saying what we want and then taking action towards it, is not new to us. We do what we say we are going to do.

But here is what happened. The first week there was daily posting of what we had done, the excitement and proud feeling that we had done something for ourselves. The photos that were shared of the walks that we went on, the reading with a cuppa, the "I can see your trainers" in the exercise photos. Then a few days of crickets... then a renewed commitment, because we know that it WORKS and we enjoyed it. It made us more productive, more creative, more able, more accountable. Then tumbleweeds for a few days. You get the picture. And I know that you will see yourself in this feeling of, "YAY new and exciting challenge... what was the challenge I was doing? I'll start it again tomorrow. Poop I missed a day. I love the challenge, I'm back on it. Crikey, was that a month??" Are you with me?

What we saw at the end of the month was that we had managed to commit to the challenge of "doing something for myself" 65–80% of the time. SCIENCE PEOPLE!

When I reflected on this, I could quite clearly see that this is how I run my business and my life. I am BRILLIANT at committing to "that thing" for about 75% of my time, my energy, my head space. At that point, I didn't know if I was angry with myself or proud of myself.

Dealing with the mind-monkeys

Firstly, I was angry, and the mind-monkeys started – you've let yourself down, but more importantly you have let the team down that you were leading; why can't you commit to 100% of what you are doing? Why did you scroll social media for an hour when you could have/ should have been meditating, reading a book, going for a walk? You are wasting the time that you DO have. You are putting pressure on yourself when you DON'T have time. You are failing if you are not prepared to do something 100%.

That last one was a biggie. You are failing if you are not prepared to do something 100%.

I felt sick. I felt sad. I felt stupid.

But never fear… perpetually positive Trudy is here. Never down for long and always willing to stand in the power pose and look to the skies for answers!

I can't stay thinking like that. I can't let my mind-monkeys have a party with their bad-mouthing-chatter. I need to gather my thoughts, gather my strength, and say SSSHHHHHH, listen to what is REALLY happening.

So, what is really happening… wait for it, this is deep… LIFE

IS FREAKIN' HAPPENING! Life and business is absolutely happening. There isn't a day that goes past that I am not DOING for the good of my clients, my business, my communities – YES, there is a day (few days??) that goes by that I don't do something good for me – NO – that isn't ideal, YES, I know that I could (and want??) to do better at that. But my (and I'm guessing this is true for you, too) learned behaviour is to put others first. I am a wonderful-work-in-progress. I don't need to get things right 100% of the time. But I do need to have awareness around where I need to improve.

Doing the challenge in the VIP membership showed me that when we, as businesswomen, commit to others, we do more for ourselves. We are able to achieve more as part of a team. We want to succeed more. We don't want to let anyone down. AND EVEN if that commitment is for 75% of the time, we are STILL doing and achieving more than we would if we were trying to do it alone.

You are not alone

Doing it alone… it sounds lonely just saying it. I know I've said it before, and it is probably on every page of my website, but we aren't meant to do any of this alone.

I ask in every podcast episode for Shine On You Crazy Daisy podcast, "what is one lesson that you have learned that every entrepreneur should know", and quite brilliantly, around 60% of the 140 authors have said "find your tribe, find your support system, don't try to do this alone".

And they say this because they are a few years into business and realise that life is hard, business is hard, but trying to work everything out by yourself is a fool's-game and takes you twice (thrice??) as long. Find the people you want to commit to seeing, talking to, sharing with, being open with, saying "do you see me?" We have had so many new businesswomen come along to our networking events, and they turn up wondering what's going to happen, why should they invest the time, what is the point... and they leave feeling inspired, motivated and YES... less alone.

I say again, it is easier to commit to YOUR team of people. Find your team of people who will help you and support you to grow – personally and in your business. Be accountable to committing to 75% of SHINING BRILLIANCE and 25% of bleugh – we all have those days, weeks, hours... minutes... it's ok, we get it.

Each January, I run The Spectacular Challenge to £1 million, and we have businesswomen from around the world joining in to be a part of the team. Why? Not because of the money. But because of the change in mindset. For this 1 month, when other people are thinking that January is the doom-n-gloom month, we're buzzing, motivated and thinking differently. We work as a team through the month, egg each other on, and get spectacularly excited at the end of each week to say what we have earned (confidentially) in that week, so that we can watch the ever-present-money-thermometer go up and up towards our million for the month.

Again... here come the stats... 60% of people in that challenge have the best January EVER – and they build on the income each year. I am very, very proud of that. Committing to thinking differently, committing to DOING differently and committing to creating a bigger and better outcome – Boom-shak-a-la!

What's your commitment?

So my question to you is: Where and how do you need to commit to yourself?

Set yourself a challenge of something and see what percentage of the time you do it for – approach it scientifically (wear a lab coat and glasses if you have any handy). Apply that percentage to everything you do – are you angry (something needs to change) or are you proud (make sure you're applying that percentage to all areas of your life).

I hear from mums all the time that they struggle with the juggle of being 100% present for their children and their businesses. YOU CAN'T DO THAT. That is so much pressure on you. You are 1 person, and you are doing your best. If the science says that you are available and willing for 75% of the time, then HASHTAG WINNING!

I know a mum in the networking group that has her desk in a closet under the stairs (I hope it is a bigger space than I am imagining!!), but when she needs that 25% she shuts the door and hides – and that is fine! Sometimes I shut the door to the kitchen / lounge wherever I'm working and pretend to be working, but really, I'm watching "Married at First Sight" with my earphones in – tee hee! 25% of absolutely no commitment – you're welcome.

Also, just to say, and I am sure you are the same, there are those times that 100% is needed in different areas, at different times, for different reasons. And when that is needed – GO FOR IT, give it some welly, give it your all, be and feel the MOST productive, accountable, and proud. Those are the times that you are seeing the growth in yourself and your business. It is the difference between working IN your business and ON your business. Find and create the time (I see the eye roll – ha ha) to commit to what you want for the future growth, and get out of your own way because change-is-a-comin'.

By the way, the mind-monkeys only have control of my brain for a very short time. I am (for the most part) proud of myself!

BIO:

Trudy Simmons is a Clarity and Productivity Business Coach for women entrepreneurs, with a truckload of empathy and a little bit of hard-arse!

She helps you find out WHAT you want to do, WHY you want to do it, and HOW to get it DONE!

She loves to show her audience how to become more successful by getting clarity, taking action, and following through. Trudy has 20 years' experience in helping people move from being stuck and not knowing the next step, to getting their shizzle DONE by finding and harnessing their strengths and removing their weaknesses!

She knows what keeps you up at night – the thousand ideas that are germinating in your brain – and she knows how to sort them into "no go", "maybe later", and "hells yes", and get done what's really important to your success.

She is the creator and founder of the Shine On You Crazy Daisy membership – which gives you the opportunity to grow your tribe, expand your audience, take in monthly knowledge, and work ON your business in online co-working and focus and accountability fortnightly group coaching.

www.thedaisychaingroup.com

2
TURNING PAIN TO POWER

La Toya Zavala

I remember the day I left my abuser. I had lived under his control and abuse for a few years. I had given up my soul, my self-worth, my dignity, my self-respect, my sovereignty over my money, time, relationships, schooling opportunities and even work schedule. My credit-worthiness was destroyed and I thought my future was too. I felt isolated, destroyed, and defeated. I had succumbed to a life that I had never imagined for myself, yet somehow found myself living. I wasn't even sure who I was and had no awareness of who I was becoming. However, on that fateful Sunday morning, I had what I call a Phoenix moment. I knew that it was my time, for the final time, to die to that self and regenerate a new self. I had no idea how, or even why, but I knew it was time. I had to go, and I did. While he was off galavanting in the car that I bought, I grabbed some clothes, threw it in a trash bag, walked out the door, and slid the key under the door. I called my brother and timidly asked him to pick me up, not knowing if he would. He did, and I began the very, very, very long and challenging road of rebuilding my life.

It's been a voyage since that hot summer Sunday in Boston, MA, in 1998. It was a long journey getting back in school and completing my BA, MDiv., Post-Graduate studies, and several certificates after. It was a long road qualifying, and then entering the U.S. Navy as an officer. It was a long road healing and building a strong marriage that has lasted more than 20 years. It has been an expedition healing and repairing my credit history and worthiness. I could go on and on...but I think you get the drift, it's been a long road! And all along this road, I've encountered some of the most bizarre and extreme male chauvinism, oppression and suppression.

I could recount to you the day I sat in class and listened to the professor tell a room full of students that women should not be in our profession and that they should go home, be teachers or be nurses. Yes, that happened. I could recount to you the day many of my male classmates surrounded me at the end of an event to tell me that there's no way I could be called to my profession as a woman. Yup, that happened. I could recount to you the day I sat in a meeting, as an officer in the Navy, and listened to my superior officer tell the room full of meeting attendees that women should stay silent, repeating it twice, with banging fists on the table. Uh-huh, that happened. I could recount to you the day I got fired from my specific duty because my male superior officer was not in favor of women leading the charge, so he sabotaged me in order to fire me. Yeah, that happened. Oh, if only the word count for this book would allow, I could recount to you so many stories and pit stops along this voyage. Let me tell you, it's been something! Yeah, but what kind of something?

Yes, much of my story has been painful, traumatic, and damaging in many ways. And when you heal, when you look within and change the lense from which you look out, you can turn your pain into power. I learned to turn my pain into power. I have learned to give my own interpretation to my story. I've learned to let my story be the power that it is. So, although my story has been many things, it's also been fire. It has been my fuel when I feel drained, tired, and out of steam. It has been my staircase to new heights of wisdom. It has been my vehicle for empathy, understanding, and connection. My story is so much of my 'why' for what I do and deciding to become an entrepreneur to do it.

You see, taking back my power, for me, included taking back authority over my soul, my self-worth, my dignity, my self-respect, my sovereignty over my money, time, relation-ships, schooling opportunities and even work schedule. For me, a very large part of that meant leaving the military and starting my own business. I absolutely loved serving some of the finest, bravest, and exceptional military personnel our world has ever known. It was my honor and privilege to help them heal from all kinds of trauma and to see them turn their pain into power. Yet, I felt limited and still subject to male chauvinism and suppression in some ways. I had to make a choice: continue in a career that I was excelling in and had a great amount of potential for rank, position, money, and opportunities - or - be and feel free on yet another level. It was a decision that I struggled with and agonized over for months. My husband and I crunched numbers and reviewed our vision for the lifestyle we wanted to have with our children over and over again. It was grueling. My peers tried to dissuade me from leaving the Navy. My pride was touched. There I was, given yet another chance to dig deep and face myself. What is the truth? What do I need in my life to continue being authentic and true to myself? What are my core values? What is my legacy to my daughter? How much do I believe in myself? Who am I?

I answered the questions. I left the Navy and became an entrepreneur.

It has most certainly not been easy and it often has been down-right scary! Becoming an entrepreneur brought up demons, triggers, and blocks that I didn't even know were still there, but I am so glad that I can see them, face them, and over-come them. Entrepreneurship has been a masterful teacher and catalyst of seeing things the way they are, and driving me to transition them to how I dream them to be. This way of life has given me the sense of freedom and power that I desired, and that I so desperately desire to give to others. It has given me the platform to create the legacy I envision leaving. It is a consum-mate connector, linking my past, my present, and my future. It's helped me release relationships with things, people, and beliefs that are no longer aligned with who I am and what I am creat-ing. It's helped me accrue allies, supporters, and mentors that would not be in my life had I not chosen this path. It opened the door to one of the most important, and soul-saving decisions my husband and I made for our family, selling all our stuff and moving to Portugal. Even if I had all the space, time, and words to tell you what the decision to become an entrepreneur has done for me and my family, I don't know that I could do it justice.

No one can have absolute grasp on what the future holds. And definitely, things shift. What I do know is that my success is part of my legacy. When my 4-year old daughter, and other young girls like her, look at me, they will see a strong, coura-geous, resilient, free, and empowered black woman who is thriving and helping as many women as she can to do the same. They will see her leading courses, speaking at events, and leading her clients to freedom, power, and victory. They will know that they can also be successful and create impact in their field and in their communities, no matter what they've been through or who they are. They will know that they too, intrinsically, are strong, courageous, resilient, free and empowered. They will know that there are no limits. They will know that they can dream. When other women who have been traumatized and are not sure if they can be entrepreneurs, or if they can take back power and authority in so many areas of their lives, they can look at La Toya Zavala and know that there are no limits.

If this is you, my most perfect soul, you can do this. You can heal and be whole again. You can have sovereignty over your life again. Entrepreneurship can help you in more ways than you know. Know that there is a sisterhood of those that have gone before you to stand by you and walk alongside you. Your future self awaits you.

I'm sending you much love and power, always.

BIO:

La Toya is a survivor-turned-thriver of domestic violence, sexual assult, and all kinds of trauma. She's turned her experience, education, training and passion into The 7C's of Power Infusion, a 7 step process including coaching, EFT and Energy Healing, to help high-achieving women release blocks and triggers from former toxic relationships so that they can know, love, trust and be themselves, activating all of their power and leaving a greater legacy. She is a lover of pizza, wine, dancing and traveling. She currently resides in Portugal with her amazing husband of over 20 years and her 3 children.

www.latoyazavala.com

3
FROM UNWANTED BABY TO POWERBABE!

Amisha Joshi-Bhardwaj

T his is my journey from the baby of the family, to head of the household at 17, to international hotel business-woman at 34.

"I NEVER wanted a 3rd child!

And when she was born, my mother cried at my fate!

"Poor you! How will you raise 3 girls?!" she asked me??

"She's born with her own destiny!"

I've never talked about this before and feel it's necessary to share this with you.

These were the words my mother said about me in nearly every single conversation with a family member - it was almost like her old cassette player was stuck and it played this dialogue on loop and she could do nothing about it.

I was born in the 70s in a Hindu Brahmin joint family in Bombay, India - a relatively modern era in a very cosmopolitan global city from its 200 year British influence.

Yet these were the attitudes of my mother, a woman who never got to fulfil her aspirations of being a basketball player.

And instead she married my dad and ended up being a homemaker rearing 3 girls!

And there I was, the last of the 3, 10 years younger than my eldest sister.

All my life I wondered if somehow, through some form of black magic (big belief in some parts of India), I had forced my father onto her and got her impregnated so that I could come into the human world!

I would hear her saying these words and feel sorry for her...the poor woman. She had to suffer because of me.

Unfortunately for my mother, my dad suddenly died when I was 17 and she was left with the responsibility of ....ME.

What ended up happening though is that I was left with the responsibility of HER...of her grief and depression of losing the only financial support in her life.

That too, while all along I felt like a burden... someone who'd just turned up uninvited and crashed her life (pun intended).

The family wanted to get me married to a 30-year-old man in the USA (I was still only 18) so that I wouldn't be a burden on my Mom.

I had to use all my might to fight such a bizarre situation from happening in my life.

The good thing though is that it fuelled the fire to become uber empowered in myself that no one in the world could ever make me feel like I am a burden.

All this eventually did take its toll on me.

I ended up keeping silent and to myself pretty much my whole life.

No matter where I went, I had this constant nagging uneasy, sticky, gluey feeling in my chest....

...that I was intruding

…that I wasn't wanted

…that no one wanted to hear what I had to say.

Before he died, my dad owned and ran a very successful finance company built by his father.

The business had very wealthy clients, some of the top businesses and corporations - the inner circle of Bombay…ones who would only wine and dine in exclusive venues, and network at the Derby horse races.

Almost all of their business events or even family ones - grand weddings or anniversary parties would take place at the Crystal Room at The Taj Mahal Mumbai - the world's most iconic hotel (also the one that was victim of the 26/11 attacks in Bombay); built in 1902 ironically by a man who wasn't allowed into a hotel by the British because he was Indian.

My dad was invited to each and every big event…and from the age of 10 onwards I tagged along…and strutted in like I owned the place just to get the special ice cream that The Taj made.

That's how I became fascinated with luxury hotels.

In my teen years as a college student, my friends and I often took our breaks from our lectures and would visit The Shamiana - the most famous Coffee shop of that time.

I would save up bus money by walking to and from college so that I could pay for my coffee and ice cream.

After my dad's sudden death, I planned to quit studying and get into the workplace (*No woman* in my family *had ever worked. Except 2 of my aunts who had migrated to the USA in the 70s and worked out of necessity*).

As an undergrad in India, the only place I could think of that employed girls was the hotel that I so often visited. I made out an application for the job of a receptionist.

But before I could send it out, my mom tore it up!

"Nothing Doing," she said. "We come form a good family and good girls don't work at hotels."

I was shocked and confused at the same time by what she meant.

I mean why would she think that I'd become a bad girl if I worked at a hotel. They all looked perfectly fine to me in all those times that I visited.

As I couldn't figure what she meant I backed down.

I went to complete my education and started working at HSBC while pursuing an MBA AND studying German alongside.

But life came full circle.

The same hotel company, the Taj Group, advertised that they were recruiting sales managers with foreign language skills....and I jumped at it!

Thereafter I spent 10 years in the corporate side of the hotel industry (not at the reception desk as I severely lacked the ability to speak to anyone given my withdrawn and silent self), managing sales and developing online distribution and revenue management - the heartbeat of how a hotel earns its money.

I was one of 5 people in the team, the only woman, and created the foundation of all internet based online hotel bookings that the company would ever do.

While I am not gloating, I had more knowledge and expertise than the collective knowledge of the other 4 members. I would be at work 6 days a week...attend MBA class in the evenings 5 days a week, German lessons on Saturdays. AND when my mom would be unwell, which was more often than not, I would go home during my lunch break to care for her and have lunch with her so she wouldn't feel lonely.

In fact it's my colleagues who christened me 'PowerBabe' based on all that I was doing and had still excelled in my career! It was then that the 'business' gene that I inherited from my dad and his dad activated itself.

I thought to myself, "if a huge company like the Taj is still grappling with this, other hotels wouldn't have a clue on what to do....so why not create a business to provide them with the tools, techniques and strategies to succeed?".

And moreover, it would give me the flexibility to stay around for my mom as needed.

I followed my gut instinct and went onto set up my own company – "Aurora", named after the northern lights.

Eventually, when I got married to my husband who was already in London, I moved the company with me.When I got pregnant, I had a lot of issues and was confined to bed rest until my son was born. While my attention was on my new baby given all the complexities of my pregnancy, my amazing husband went on to expand the business as I was attending to what was priority for me.He brought the clients in and I supported them from the back office baby in tow....and within 5 years we created a client base of over 500 hotels worldwide, supporting their business strategy and know-how with bespoke exclusive consulting and training.

Being a woman, I am sure you know that our evolution never ends...we are always aspiring for more, for greater stuff.

Just supporting the clients from home wasn't enough...it wasn't satisfying or fulfilling. I loved being a mum and being fully present for my son. But I also wanted to be in the action... in the spotlight...in front of hotel teams, empowering and motivating them.

By then I was certified as an NLP Trainer and a Coach.This inspired me to create EMOTIONAL FITNESS MASTERY - coaching women in and outside of the hotel industry to BE THAT WOMAN and achieve - despite the odds.Why this you may ask? So that we can move past our emotional barriers and break out of biases. The barriers we unknowingly created through our life's experiences. The biases that we've inherited through the beliefs of those around us...those who influenced us knowingly or unknowingly.

MAGIC HAPPENS when we overcome emotional barriers

about what is good, what isn't good....what we can and what we can't do...and more importantly, WHO WE CAN BE AND WHO WE CAN'T.

So my message to every woman is that there will be times when you feel

Unwanted

Unloved

Unworthy

Uncared for

But nothing could be further from your truth.

There is always a way and there will always be a WIN-WIN solution to EVERYTHING. So start winning no matter what or who says you can't because THAT'S your true destiny!

So go on and unleash the Powerbabe in you.

BIO:

Amisha, a certified Trainer of Neuro Linguistic Programming [NLP] and an Emotional Fitness Coach, and is the founder of Emotional Fitness Mastery.She grew up in Bombay, India and has lived in London for 15 years. She has spent twenty years in the hotel industry. Amisha's life mission is to empower women with Emotional Fitness so they can truly BE THAT WOMAN that they always wanted to be but never knew HOW. She helps not just hotel industry professionals, but also individuals overwhelmed by life's challenges, to overcome their emotional barriers and make space for magic.

Her motto is "I believe there is a win-win solution for everything."

She is a regular speaker at the GLOBAL NLP SUMMIT and has been featured on Ticker News - Australia and BBC 5 Live

www.IAMEmotionallyFit.com

4
RECLAIMING YOUR FORWARD MOVEMENT

Wendy Welpton

Sometimes your 'why' comes and grabs you when you least expect it!

Flashback to look forward.

"A natural movement coach? Who, me? You must be joking! What's natural movement anyway, I've never even heard of it!"...would have been my first response if you'd told me 10 years ago what I'd be doing in my life now.

My second response would have been, "I can't coach, I haven't got any experience! I'm an ex-Marketeer, a mum!". I would have been amused at the thought and asked how on earth I would get there?!

Your answer would have been that 2 years from then, at 40 years of age, I would have to stop my beloved running and my movement ability would be drastically reduced for 4 years whilst I struggled through chronic pain. Out of kindness you might not have told me about the far more challenging emotional rollercoaster I would ride, and the level of hard work I would have to put in, to get back to anywhere near the level of movement confidence I had then. Clearly, I wouldn't have wanted to believe you. I'm thankful we can never see the future!

My 'why', although I didn't know it at the time

So, what happened at 40? The strange thing is that I didn't have a specific accident or traumatic event. I've often felt my situation would have felt more valid if I had. Instead my body just finally said 'stop'!

One night after a glorious 10k run under blue skies in December 2014, I woke in the middle of the night in agony, hardly able to walk and wondered what on earth was going on. Looking back, I'd been ignoring many signs that my body was telling me something wasn't right. As I was able to walk and wasn't an urgent case, I was given strong painkillers and sent on my way by the medical world. What then followed was 4 years of chronic pain, frustration and a journey of discovery about why my body had failed me and how I was going to deal with it. I thought it would be a few months before I was back to running again, but this was certainly not the case.

Living with chronic pain, day in and day out, sabotages your life. Some days are better, with increased hope and others are rock bottom after a flare up, with hopes of recovery dashed. The physical pain would often be hard to bear, upsetting and exhausting, but I found the mental challenge the most difficult by far. Chronic pain is like a subconscious brain obsession where you find yourself checking in all day long, without even wanting to. It dominates everything. I often wondered whether I would ever get back to myself again or thought was this the 'new me'?

I found my way through by researching, taking a deep-dive to give me some answers. I found out more about how bodies work. With therapists, I worked out why it had happened to me, which movements didn't serve me and which would always be needed. The final step was to surrender difficult emotions in order to accept what was happening and it was at this point, my recovery really started to progress. I now truly believe that mind and body affect each other hugely and have to work together for the best outcomes.

To cut a very long story short(er), I found out, years later, that I am hypermobile, meaning my ability to keep my body in good alignment is harder than for those without this condition. As a result of many years of sitting (badly) at a desk and then carrying my 3 boys (both inside and out!), my body alignment was all over the place. I then added the impact forces of my beloved running and my muscles could no longer take up the strain for my overlax ligaments and a vicious cycle of pain ensued.

Dare to dream

Fast forward to 2017 and gradual improvements in my levels of pain. I started to see a life without pain as a possibility. My deep-dive had made me realise that having chosen GCSE German (well, actually O'Levels in Scotland way back then!) over Biology, meant I had a missing chunk of knowledge about the human body. Having ignited a renewed thirst for learning, I decided to set my first challenge. I studied for an Anatomy & Physiology qualification and amazed myself by getting Distinction.

I accepted that running was unlikely to serve me for the rest of my years and as my pain slowly reduced through rehabilitation work and my confidence and hope grew, I realised I needed to find a way of moving that would challenge me and keep me strong. Through my research into bodies and movement, I stumbled across something called, 'natural movement'.

This was when Katy Bowman, founder of 'Nutritious Movement', appeared on my horizon. Everything she said made so much sense to me. Her way of living and moving through life was about embracing the range of movements we're born with, but that we don't use in the modern world due to the introduction of life's conveniences and comforts. I read, listened and watched everything I could. I then had the good fortune to meet her in person. She pointed me in the direction of MovNat; a system for retraining the body by going back to early developmental movement patterns to re-educate the nervous system. The overlap with my rehabilitation movements made me realise this could be a way I could move for the rest of my life to counteract my issues with hypermobility, keeping me strong whilst being mobile.

I decided to work towards a certification as a personal challenge and to give my training and recovery a focal point. After much studying and practise, I passed in September 2019 and it was one of the most proud (and exhausting) moments in my life. It felt like I had finally got past one of the hardest chapters of my life and I felt great, both physically and mentally!

Looking back now, I actually see my years in pain as a lucky wake up call. My body gave me a stern warning that I could end up going down a path I never expected to take, a warning many don't listen to until it's too late or ignore for as long as they can. I felt like I flashed forward to 80 at the age of 40 and I was scared by what I saw. I realised I had to prioritise my body's movement patterns for the rest of my life and that others needed to do the same. This was to be the catalyst for the next exciting, and often frightening, chapter!

Who, me, coach? Why not?!

I decided to launch a natural movement coaching business to fulfil what I now realised was my purpose; to help others avoid what had happened to me and to share the knowledge I'd gained, whilst also helping me to keep moving! I only whispered this idea to my closest friends and even then I told them it was probably just a pipe dream. I didn't want to create any expectation and, fearing failure, didn't want to put my head above the parapet! I had always dreamt of setting up a business and have entrepreneurs all around me in my family. I put lots of time and effort into a few previous attempts, but none of them came to anything. With hindsight, I was 'looking' for an idea, instead of the idea finding me! Each experience taught me something new and made me more ready when I finally got going. 2020 brought lockdown and my plans for setting up my business had to change. I was coaching friends and family for free to gain experience and shape my class offering, and had to switch to do so online. The ongoing pandemic made this a permanent feature. I soon realised that although there were many parts to natural movement that required greater space and equipment, it was in fact the foundational ground movement work that people really responded to. It was a key movement ingredient missing in many people's lives. This worked well online and even better from the comfort of people's own homes.

From movement coach to business owner, social media manager to so many more roles!

I have always felt grateful I have a marketing background as it has helped me in so many ways. However, my first career in marketing ended when Facebook was the big new thing! I can even admit to a rather drunken argument with friends, saying I would 'never' be on Facebook as these people couldn't all really be called 'Friends'! For the sake of my business I had to get off my soapbox to harness the power and embrace the possibilities of social media. I had to bite the bullet and just go for it! Although I still feel uncomfortable talking directly to the camera, I've now done so many things that were so far out of my comfort zone, that each time those new experiences get easier and I realise I am growing. I have even found that I actually enjoy making content for social media as I find it a great creative outlet, as well as a useful platform to communicate my message of how natural movement has helped me, what it's all about and how it could help my audience. The bonus, that I never expected, was the sense of community, support and encouragement from people whom I've mostly never met, but who share a common purpose.

Setting up your own business requires so much more than just marketing skills. As in my journey through pain, progression has always come from keeping an open mind, listening, reading, researching and most importantly by talking to others in the same position. Every step forward can feel like a massive leap of faith where you either end up beaming with pride, or falling down and having to dust yourself off, learn lessons about your business and yourself, and then get up and start walking again. It's easy to forget your wins, so I write down all the things that go well, no matter how small. I also write down the things that go wrong and try to learn from them. This small business journaling has served me well. Looking back helps me to look forward with greater confidence; something I now realise my time in pain took from me in many ways.

Living, learning and moving forwards, every day!

I've had to challenge myself to do things that have felt very uncomfortable, but every time I learn and grow. I aim to keep improving my coaching. When a client recently said, "you haunt me" when talking about her newfound awareness of her daily movement, it was actually the biggest compliment she could have given me; my goal is to inspire lifelong change, even in the smallest ways. I am also moving into education to increase awareness of the benefits of embracing natural movement to improve our lives. I now know that you really can learn to do anything you want to, if your reason for doing it is strong enough!

BIO:

Wendy founded Reclaim Movement in 2020 to help people embrace a movement-rich life to move well for life and do the things they love. Wendy is a MovNat Certified Trainer who shows people ways to incorporate regular movement breaks into their daily lives and how to use their bodies in healthy movement patterns. Her goal is to help people reclaim the natural movement skills they were born with, to avoid injury, improve mobility and stay strong. Wendy shares ideas on social media, coaches online movement group classes and privately, hosts an On Demand video library and holds educational workshops.

www.reclaimmovement.co.uk

LIFE REALLY IS A
ROLLERCOASTER

Hannah Roper

Well where to start, as a lover of all things musical theatre, I will take inspiration from Julie Andrews in *The Sound Music* and 'start at the very beginning, as it's a very good place to start'.

I have had a varied employed career, starting on the deli counter at Waitrose, moving to a record shop (yep real life vinyl records, and we had old style VHS rentals too!), barmaid (back in the day when people bought you drinks all night), learning assistant, secondary school music teacher, primary school teacher, police officer, and learning and development consultant! I am also a mum, wife, and general life project manager, so have worn many hats in my life!

So how does this relate to business I hear you ask!

Whilst working as a police officer in 2014, I had made the brave decision to leave my abusive marriage. For 8 years I had been subjected to coercive and controlling abuse tactics resulting in a complete lack of self-worth and confidence. One day I had reached my enough-is-enough point and with nothing more than my handbag and my 4 year son, I walked out the door on 7th January 2014. Having suffered domestic abuse, I found myself struggling more and more with being a police officer; it was hampering my recovery process, so I started to look at other options.

As a form of therapy I had begun to write music. It was a way for me to process the trauma and find myself again — cheesy I know! I was encouraged to share my songs with friends and family, and before I knew it, I was performing in public and looking at making a short album!

The response I was getting for my music provided me with the validation I needed and helped rebuild my confidence; however, to be able to perform after the abuse I suffered was only made possible through creating a character, Lily Garland. She was my equivalent to Beyonce's Sasha Fierce, and she provided a protective shield around me to give me space to process where I had come from and where I wanted life to go in the future. It also allowed me to keep this new passion away from the stresses and strains of being in the police and put a strong boundary around it.

Through Lily Garland, I regained my passion for performing and music after leaving it all behind when I met my first husband, and soon I had my sights set on the iTunes charts! But to get into the charts, my music had to be downloaded by lots of people — why would they do that when they didn't know I existed? This began my professional relationship with social media and PR!

I had to learn how to use social media and PR opportunities to promote myself, connect with my audience, and encourage not only music downloads but also attendance at my performances! It was a steep learning curve I can tell you!

But as with everything I threw myself fully into it, I started to understand the purpose of social media, learnt how to create a brand, and launched my first ever website. As time went on, I learnt more and more about SEO, PR, and branding, as I enjoyed it so much.

Between 2015 and 2020 I released 3 EPs, appeared in numerous interviews on audio and visual online platforms (who knew this was a skill that I would learn to develop and really enjoy), received multiple published glowing reviews, and performed across the UK. I also received multiple award nominations, including 2 winning accolades (which I still proudly display in my office); had a line of Lily Garland merchandise; facilitated my own headline gigs; and created my own 3 day country music festival, Country on the Coast, which launched in April 2019 and made a profit in the first year!

Now I knew the music world was not going to make the level of income I needed to break free from working for the police. Through therapy, I had come to the conclusion that I could never truly heal until I removed myself from this environment, but to do that I needed another income.

A friend of mine, whom I knew through amateur dramatics, had been sharing her business venture on Facebook. She was a network marketing consultant for a large health and wellness company, also called social selling. I didn't know anything about that.

The turning point came when I was in a stage of feeling incredibly unhealthy, and in October 2017 I was diagnosed with high blood pressure. It was time to take charge of my life so at the end of 2017, I contacted my friend about the healthy eating programme she was running. To say the results were life changing is an understatement, but not necessarily in the way you would think! This healthy eating programme finally exposed a long time set of digestive issues, which turned out to be coeliac disease, the autoimmune condition in which all gluten containing products need to be cut out, for life! So for that I will be forever thankful!

This also led to me finding out more about the business model of network marketing. I loved the company products, used them daily, and recommended them naturally, so it made sense to jump in and become a consultant myself.

Through this experience, I was plunged into a world where women truly championed each other. Never had I seen so many inspirational women in one space, not only striving for financial independence, but also embracing personal development and becoming clear on their vision for the future.

During this time, I increased my experience with using social media, but I found it difficult to stand out from the crowd. It was clearer for Lily Garland; however, in this forum there were lots of people, like me, promoting the same products.

I took the decision to invest in personal branding training. I learnt so much about identifying my ideal client, creating a persona, and using social media to create content that speaks to them. I put all the theory into practice, and my confidence continued to grow.

Network marketing didn't work out for me. I made a small income, but nowhere near what I needed to make. I also felt that in the age of social media, network marketing needed to take another approach; those who were successful in this business model were more influencer-like. I didn't want that pressure, nor could I look perfect all the time, so that chapter closed.

But I will be forever thankful, as I had the opportunity to discover the person I knew I wanted to be. Also, I grew in confidence and self-belief. During this time I met my now husband and left the police in 2018 for a role in a large aviation firm.

But that is not the end of my story because along came Covid …

Yep that's right, I cannot tell my story without talking about the Global Pandemic of 2020. In terms of business, everything just stopped. I could no longer perform as Lily Garland, the music festival was postponed, and I was furloughed from the job I loved.

After a small pity party, I found a community of mums, most of whom lived locally to me. We would meet online in between homeschooling to share our moans, gratitude, and new experiences, such as journaling and calligraphy. I discovered a creative side of myself outside of music, something I didn't know was there.

There was a lot of talk about side hustles, with many women wanting to leave the day job, not return after maternity leave, or bring in a bit of extra income due to the instability of the pandemic. I was in a lucky position in that my job was relatively secure, my income was unaffected, and I was able to enjoy time at home with my son and step-daughter, but you've seen how busy I like to be, so the idea of not doing anything filled me with dread!

I saw a gap in the knowledge that these women had when it came to using social media to connect with their audience. They were unaware of the power of branding and how to set up the right business foundations to make an income, so what does someone who needs a new project that can be run remotely from home do? They fill that gap! I pulled on all the knowledge and experience I had gained through the music, festival, and network marketing and had a moment of realisation of how much value I could provide to this audience!

I set up my limited company, The Female Creative in 2020, created my branding, designed my website, and set my business plan and priorities. My focus was on supporting mums in turning their hobby into an income generating hustle, so I started to run workshops focussing on how to identify an ideal client and how to brand and market a business using social media. I helped women create branding aesthetics and websites, and gave advice on how to set up, financially manage, and determine the right activities for their business. This fulfilled the creative hole left by the music and gave me an inspired purpose to get through the series of lockdowns and restrictions.

I invested in a business development coach in the summer of 2020. I wanted to become even clearer in what I offered and create a business that I could balance alongside my day job when the furlough period was over. It was the best investment I had ever made.

As the needs of my audience changed during the uncertain times we were in, my business flexed, and I added a monthly membership to provide a more consistent support option alongside the 121 approach. When I returned to my aviation role in September 2021, I reduced my capacity for 121 coaching and mentoring, continued running the group membership, but also added a podcast and networking events to my marketing strategy.

I continued to learn more and more skills in business management and marketing, including PR which I was then able to implement in the strategy for my music festival, Country on the Coast. I have appeared in media features, guest blogs, radio interviews, social media collaborations; given talks; and received two award nominations. I feel so thankful. These skills also made me a better learning and development professional, and I am currently working on a framework to incorporate learning and marketing strategies to enhance training in organisations.

To bring this part of my story to its conclusion, I can't bypass the personal transformation that running The Female Creative has brought to my life. I was able to remove the protective shield that Lily Garland had provided for so long. I was able to stand up as myself, share my experiences and expertise, and no longer care so deeply about what people thought of me —not completely, but we're all human right?! I am finally becoming the person who my children can be proud of, and who I can be proud of too!

BIO:

Hannah Roper, founder and director of The Female Creative, is a coach, mentor and community creator for female business owners. Drawing on over 20 years' experience in learning and development and 7 years' as an entrepreneur, Hannah provides solutions for growth, activity prioritisation, organisation, and self-confidence for small business owners through 121 coaching, a group membership, and networking events, and as a podcast host for The Female Creative Talks. Hannah has recently received an accolade for Top Female Business Coaches Worldwide 2022 from Coach Foundation and was the recipient for the Pamodzi Inspirational Women of Portsmouth Awards 2022 in the Established Business Category.

www.thefemalecreative.co.uk

6

FINDING YOUR ALIGNED SUCCESS

Zuzana Taylor

I grew up in Slovakia; creative and curious, ambitious, and passionate. I loved helping people from an early age. My parents, especially my dad, constantly reminded me that only I could make my life better and only I was responsible for how my life shaped up… I could do anything I dreamed of!

I remember clearly how serious he was and that he REALLY meant it. He wasn't joking as he usually would… it was almost like my life depended on this. I could FEEL the importance of it, and it was scary! This one-way conversation with my dad has stayed with me until today.

I created this belief system that only I can make things happen; nobody else will do it for me.

I'm grateful to my dad for this powerful experience. It made me who I am, shaping my life path and purpose.

As life continued, I moved to London, studied Psychology, and had a career working in business and marketing.

I also met my husband and started a family. Having my two children and becoming a mum was another extremely powerful experience.

During this time, the need to fulfil my own creativities and passions grew much stronger, and it wasn't a coincidence it happened when I had my children. Because, as women, we're strongly connected with our inner creative feminine side.

But deep down, amongst that love and devotion for my children, I felt something was missing.

It was time for me to think about going back to work, but I had a strong pull to follow the calling inside me. It was beautiful yet painful and scary. I felt my purpose calling me to do what I'm here to do and that my children should see that. Otherwise, what's the point? What legacy am I going to leave behind?

But at the same time, all sorts of guilty questions ran through my head...

"You got what you wanted. You have two beautiful children".

"You're so ungrateful. Look at the women that can't have children. They would be so happy."

"What's wrong with you? You have everything".

Having children IS the most beautiful and rewarding gift, but it can leave you feeling

you've given up on your own dreams and lost your identity.

I didn't follow that powerful inner voice. Instead, I carried on trying to be grateful for what I had. I powered through, but all those desires I tried to push away became stronger until I broke down one day. I remember it well; sitting in the kitchen with my head on the table crying. My husband found me and I couldn't even say what had happened.

But it was the BEST thing that could've happened. Because we talked, and I angrily but honestly said what I REALLY wanted. I couldn't see how to make it happen straight away, but I had a deep belief in my calling to help other mums.

I craved the freedom to work to my own schedule, and it

became clear the time had come to work for myself. I wanted the flexibility to be around my two small children, enjoy every special moment with them, yet continue my passions for business, marketing and psychology.

I've always been drawn to people and the way they work. I started to see my calling was to help and support other mums to harness their power, follow their dreams, start their own business and create the life they desire.

I wanted it all! So, I decided to create it!

I took this powerful experience into my own hands and made it happen. I combined my love for psychology and mindset with my extensive experience in business and marketing, as well as understanding the challenges being a mother brings.

For three years, I helped my clients build successful businesses through bespoke coaching programmes, whilst growing my own strength, confidence, connection, and purpose. Everything was in a nice flow.

Until last year, when things didn't feel right. I was heading in the wrong direction.

I thought I had it all... a successful business serving and helping my ideal clients. But I still wasn't feeling the connection. Something powerful was missing but I couldn't figure out what it was.

During this time, I launched two group coaching programmes. Both failed and the consistent stream of clients I was used to disappeared.

I was going round in circles. I knew I needed to let go of the attachments that kept me in the rat race. I was talking about it; I was aware of it but I couldn't stop it.

Then last year, during the global pandemic, my beautiful mum suddenly passed away. It was a massive shock to me and the whole of my family. Suddenly everything stopped. I stopped. There was no way I could carry on with my rat race anymore.

I had to travel to Slovakia for my mum's funeral. But I also had to leave my two children and husband behind. As a daughter, I was torn and deeply wounded. I was alone because my mum wasn't there anymore. But I was a mother too, and I had this incredible strength to ensure my children were safe and looked after whilst I was away.

As you can imagine, with all the stress, pain and sadness, I created this huge protection around me and connected with love, which carried me through.

I remember my friend from London calling me to offer support, and I said, *"It's so powerful, I'm being guided."*

I felt more than before, all the different energies around me, and I could choose which one to go into. I chose love because that's exactly what I needed to heal my wound. But I also had this empowering moment where I clearly saw how I harnessed and controlled this powerful energy. THIS is my unique gift!

From that moment, I felt I was being guided. An enormous higher power of gratitude was pouring through me. There was this instance when I needed a car to organise my mum's funeral. My brother's friend who I hardly knew offered me their car, so we had a car... miracle! The energy of the universe was present. I felt it and trusted it. There were many restrictions during the COVID pandemic, but people were going far and above to help. Everything worked out the way I wanted it... but better.

I came out of this higher experience, re-connected with my true self and higher purpose... and the endless, enormous power and belief that was aligned with my gift to help others.

My intuition guided me on this journey. I became unstoppable. Free to speak about who I am, do things my way, and live my life on my own terms. Free to create success that's aligned with me and my family.

It became apparent the missing piece was the connection with my true authentic self and purpose. My whole life slotted together like puzzle pieces. Finally, it all made sense and I could see it happening. Everything I ever wanted and dreamed of in my life, I now have!

There's no limit to success. YOU are your own limit, and that's why once you unleash your true self, you can achieve anything and everything.

Yes, you need the strategies and mindset work, but it's you that people connect with... the energy that shines through you. Once you harness it, it's like a magnet. Dream opportunities will start coming your way without you making a big effort.

Once you decide to make things happen and commit to it, you'll have it all... you'll create a beautiful flow of abundance.

Follow your intuition and strengthen your mindset because it's all connected.

You are your business. You are the person behind it all. You make things happen. Once you reach one level of success, you enter the next, and that's how you grow and evolve.

The secret to your aligned success is YOU and how you do things authentically by being your true self. Be led and empowered by your intuition because that's your unique strength.

Get out of your own way and be YOU, because the unique gift you have is your secret path to SUCCESS! (and everything else you can figure out!)

All the powerful breakthroughs that led me to my next level of success happened when I followed my intuition and connected with who I am.

Intuition is the voice of your soul, and your soul holds the answers for the happiness you want. Your soul knows what makes you happy!

To find your truth, dig deep into your subconscious and your soul. Writing can help bring your true gifts up to the surface. (It's how I created my first poem, 'MAMA'.)

Remember, only you have the power to make your dreams happen. There's no such thing as "I'll do it tomorrow" because there might not be tomorrow! Time is the only thing you

DON'T have, so do something every day that takes you one step closer to your dreams.

Give yourself permission to step back and re-connect. You won't lose anything; you'll gain more than you can ever imagine!

My powerful journey has led me to where I am today... helping female entrepreneurs connect with their true selves and follow their intuition, so they can build successful businesses and lives aligned with their values.

My journey hasn't always been like a beautiful walk on rose petals... more the opposite! But I love this because it made me stronger and more connected with my true self. I'm fulfilling all my dreams in a way that sometimes I have to stop and pinch myself that it's actually happening in real life. And I'm so grateful!

Things aren't always easy. There are challenges, but I'm on my path and I love it! It keeps my ambitions alive and drives me forward to reach the next levels in business and life.

What's different now is I know my gift helps others. My inner strength carries me through the challenges. I'm in control and decide what I do with them... whether they'll take me closer to my dream. I own my true voice that connects with the right people and I'm not afraid to speak up. I know my purpose and have a mission aligned with my life. I also have all the business tools and knowledge, and amazing opportunities flow my way because of it.

I truly wish the same for you.

When I'm successful, my clients are too... and that creates a huge ripple effect that makes a difference in the world.

Because everything is energy, and we're all connected. (Choose very carefully who and where you give your energy!)

I have trust that I have the power to create and fulfil all my dreams. I'm grateful and love the freedom to be in the present moment, with everything it brings.

I'll continue to show up in my own way, serve my clients, lead with my heart, take risks, invest in myself, and commit to doing what I'm on this planet to do!

BIO:

Zuzana Taylor is a transformational business coach and heart-led mentor.

She helps intuitive female entrepreneurs step into their next level of aligned success, connect with their true selves and regain their confidence, so they can build a business and life they love... whilst staying aligned with their core values and true calling in the world.

Zuzana offers tailored 1:1 coaching, and a signature group programme based on her '10 Powerful Pillars to Your Aligned Success'.

She also offers a safe space for intuitive women inside her free Facebook group, 'Unleash Your True Self'.

www.zuzanataylor.com

7

YOU ARE NOT EVERYONE'S CUP OF TEA

Eloho Efemuai

I used to think that my self-worth depended on what others thought or said about me and for years I struggled to fit in. I was an approval addict. Though I desired to make a positive lasting impact on the lives of the people I met, I felt stuck and like a lid was placed over me.

Because of the abuse and rejection I suffered, I desperately wanted everyone to like me or approve of me and the things I did. So, I did everything I could to please any and everyone not even caring how that was affecting me personally, my family, my ministry and even my business.

Even though I looked like this strong woman on the outside who had it all together, who knew what she was doing, who was flying people from all over the world to her concerts and had built the fastest growing online radio station in Scotland, on the inside I was battling my own little demons and begging for attention.

I didn't recognise my own worth, I didn't even value myself, how did I expect others to value me and see the worth in me. I sold myself short.

My confidence, any little I had, was badly hit, my self-esteem was so low, and I battled with imposter syndrome. I thought everyone else was better than me, everyone else had it all together and knew what they were doing but me, I felt like I didn't matter, I didn't deserve to be in the room. I thought I needed to be fixed.

These beliefs, misconceptions and expectations that were placed on me and that I also placed on myself as a woman of faith, singer, radio broadcaster and woman in business, held me back from truly living and building an impactful brand. I heard words like "you shouldn't be", or "you ought to" I even told myself "This is not for people like me". When I told someone I ran an online radio station they looked at me like I was a joke and said "oh you're a radio dj" like I couldn't run my own radio station. Another person told me that they thought I was just heading the U.K. chapter of the charity I founded to host concerts. All of these held me back from truly living.

I kept going round the same circle over and over again, making the same mistakes, feeling stuck, couldn't scale and genuinely thought I had a problem until I got fed up and sought help. It's ok to ask for help, it's not a sign of weakness.

Thankfully today I am not that woman who is desperately seeking approval and wanting to please everyone. I am not everyone's cup of tea, and I am building a brand that is not just visible, but a memorable brand that actually pays. Since reclaiming my worth and dealing with the stereotypes, I have been featured on channel 4's come dine with me, the People's Friend, the Sunday post, and the Daily Records. I chose to believe in myself and see the worth in me.

Now I am so delighted to be helping other women of faith

like me, who feel like they have to shrink to build visible and impactful brands.

How I got my Groove Back and dealt with the stereotypes

First things first, I had to go back to the one who made me, the one who called me and gave me all the gifts and talents I possess to find out exactly who I was, why He made me and what He thought of me. I was reminded of my value and my worth. I was reminded of my identity. If you do not know who you are, the world will tell you and that was exactly what was happening to me.

I then chose to invest in myself and hired a coach. I joined a mastermind and found a supportive community who saw the worth in me, and then I began to thrive. To build a visible brand or business, you need community.

Slowly I began to see that there was so much more to me despite all of the rejection, the pain, the mistakes, the abuse, the betrayal I had been through. I had been seeking approval from people who didn't even have approval to give me.

To beat the stereotypes and build a visible and impactful brand you've got to realise that YOU ARE NOT EVERYONE's CUP OF TEA! You have not been sent to everyone. Not everyone will get you and that's ok, not everyone will do business with you and that's ok too. Not everyone will buy your product or service and that is ok.

If you want to stand out and be memorable, you've got to overcome the need to be liked, it can be difficult as everyone desires to be loved. But you've got to be intentional about this knowing that you belong in the space where you are.

You've got to believe that you are good enough and what you have is good enough. You need to stop second guessing yourself and believe that the service you provide is needed.

Then you need to realise that everyone is still trying to

figure it out, give yourself grace, forgive yourself, make mistakes yes but do not let those mistakes define you. Learn as you go, evolve through the process, perfect it as you go. Do it afraid. Feel the fear but do it anyway.

Realise that the stereotypes will always be there but decide to show up anyway, because it is your responsibility to let those you have been called to, know that you are there and that you have been sent to help them. Cos if you don't, you will be depriving them of the value that you bring.

Next find a supportive community, no (wo)man is an island, we all need a cheerleading squad. If you find out that the community where you are doesn't serve you, find one that does. I had to do this a few times. The process is never easy, but you've got the strength for it, you just don't realise yet. You're stuck because this is all you've ever known.

I've learnt through my journey to celebrate others and cheer them on. They may or may not celebrate you but according to a Huna Philosophy "Bless that which you want".

If you desire to make an impact, build a visible and profitable brand or business, find out who has been on the same journey or niche you are in and celebrate them. When you do, you attract this into your life.

You may have been badly hit, raped, abused, rejected but there's so much to you, if despite all I had to deal with, I have built an amazing brand, then you too can recover and build whatever you desire to build.

You are not everyone's cup of tea, stop doubting your potential, you might not even be a cup of tea, but just remember that there's someone out there who loves hot chocolate or coffee, focus on these kinds of people.

BIO:

Eloho Efemuai is a brand visibility coach, singer, speaker, author and radio broadcaster who inspires creatives and women of faith to stop doubting their potential, unleash their inner confidence by beating the stereotypes to create a 360-degree visible and impactful brand.

She runs Scotland's Number One Online Christian Radio station Heartsong Live in Edinburgh. You can find her broadcasting words of inspiration every Monday to Thursday morning from 6:30am.

As a professional singer who's released two studio albums, she's attracted an equally impressive tribe, drawn to her soulful voice and positive messages. Across her social media channels, she has almost 60-thousand fans, who engage with her on a regular basis.

Achieving such impressive follower numbers within just a few years has meant that word has spread rapidly about Eloho's social media expertise and her ability to inspire and empower women of faith to discover their true potential.

As a John Maxwell Certified coach her desire is to add value to the lives of those she encounters, particularly women who struggle with a lack of confidence and low self-esteem, helping them break out of stereotypes to become the women they were designed to be.

www.elohoefemuai.co.uk

8

TAKING ONE STEP AT A TIME

Teresa Barker

My love of sewing and then crafting started at an early age and has grown to be a real passion. The level of enjoyment I get in creating unique items makes me so happy and fulfilled. It all began at school, where I learned the basic introduction to sewing, which developed into gaining some formal qualifications in dress making so I have been able to make many sets of curtains, bedding, cushions and items of clothing over the years with fantastic results. My crafting has been a natural progression in realising my creative talents.

In 1996 I met my future husband; Rick and we were married in April 1999. I was able to fulfil one of my dreams; I made my own wedding dress and my bridesmaids' dresses. I really was very pleased with myself and felt amazing on our wedding day.

Cross Stitch for me, went hand in hand with sewing and was a natural progression to further my crafting skills and when I introduced this to my Grandma, she also fell in love with this unique way of creating beautiful things. I have many pictures that she had made for me, which are great reminders of her and our many happy hours spent together sewing, chatting and drinking tea. Crafting allows generations to achieve a very personal connection and make something together which can leave you with heirlooms to hand down to future family members and share the stories of how and when they were created. Talking of heirlooms, fast forward many years to Christmas 2021; myself, my 14-year-old son Mark, his Grandma and Grandad made a 3D Crystal Art Christmas scene. My son loved doing this and will remind him of a happy memory and the lovely time he had.

Now rewind back; I was working full time after college however I found time to craft, although I always wished I had more hours. I also wished this would be a larger part of my life instead of the mundane (to me at least) office work that I started as a career path. But crafting was in my blood and being able to buy an embroidery machine gave me a new imaginative outlet. Anything and everything I found, I tried to embroider. The obsession with embroidered items held no bounds with flannels and clothing and a whole host of different cloths coming under the needle. The enjoyment of decorating towels with a beautifully coloured teddy and their name for newborn additions of friends and family, was very fulfilling and rewarding as they had an item I had made!

An extension of sewing and needlecraft is knitting. I can't even guess how many jumpers and cardigans (and coats for my elderly dogs), my needles have conjured out of a beautiful mix of soft yarns whilst relaxing in the evening.

I have explored a variety of different office based employment roles; admin officer in Industrial Insurance, Directors PA, Administrator for a Refugee Housing and also a Foster Care Organisation. Although I enjoyed these jobs, the one thing I really wanted was to be a mum. So nearly 14 years ago, my husband and I decided to adopt. Enter two boys, aged 8 years old and 16 months, and overnight our lives changed! Our youngest, although we didn't know when we adopted him, has been diagnosed with Autism, ADHD and Tourettes. Needless to say my hobby took a back seat although I did make Mark some weighted blankets which helped him a lot. But it was quite a few years before I started crafting again and then only in small doses as everything had to be put away at the end of each session. After having the boys for a few years I found employment in our local Primary School, where our eldest son was a pupil and our youngest entering Year R. The really lovely thing for me, was that our boys were attending the Primary School I started at as a schoolgirl many moons ago.

As a result of having my creative talents restricted, my wonderful husband offered to build me a uniquely amazing workshop as it was extremely frustrating packing and unpacking the multitude of items I had accumulated. A lot of sweat and tears went into the build, but gradually it took shape and finally I could move in ... and this is where my dream started. I could start a project and leave it out until it was finished. I could even lock the door!! I had room to keep my sewing machines up and could easily see the stock I had. Bliss!! The offer to have a bed installed was declined.

My hobby was ticking along nicely and having My Shed meant I could experiment with various creative styles. I started small, mainly with unique cards and a few clothes alterations for close friends and family which then grew into setting up an Etsy shop. As my workshop is a luxury "shed" in the back garden, the name TheGiftShedCreations seemed to fit well. I started gradually expanding more items in my portfolio, like fabric bunting, kindle/tablet cushion stands and memo/notice boards and various other items. Some worked, some didn't feel right, but I was learning and exploring.

When Mark moved onto Secondary School, I had to resign

from my job to give me the flexibility as a primary carer, mother and wife. This gave me the ideal opportunity to increase my crafting and sewing time. I started to take on sewing jobs and increased the variety of products on my Etsy shop which was ticking along nicely but I wanted more.

My husband, Rick, is ex-Army and served in the REME. In 2018 he decided to take part in a sponsored walk for the ABF The Soldiers Charity and they are the Army's national charity, assisting soldiers, past and present, and their families for life. The ABF stand at the forefront of support for the Army family, last year supporting 60,000 people in 63 countries around the world. When they hear of a person in need, they aim to respond within 48 hours. Last year the youngest person they supported was two years old and the eldest 103 years young. They are there for the Army family when they need them. They offer support in six key areas: independent living, elderly care, education and employment, mental fitness, families and housing.

The sponsored walk in France and Belgium was 100km covering battlefields and cemeteries in three days. Rick took part in both 2018 and 2019 walks and was planning on taking part in one for 2020. Then we all know what happened next, Covid hit. Rick decided to sign up for the 2021 walk but instead of doing just one sponsored walk, he decided to do both. The first walk tackling the Normandy Beaches, a little break, then back to France for the Western Front starting at Lochnagar Crater, ending at the humbling Menin Gate for the Last Post. I had a lightbulb moment. I decided to donate 20% from each of my sales to the ABF. I started offering to make fabric masks which kick-started my fundraising and to date I have made over 1200 masks and raised over £1500 for my efforts. I am so proud of this achievement. Rick completed both walks but has decided to have a year off in 2022. So, guess what, I decided I am walking the challenging Western Front whilst continuing to raise funds for this wonderful charity. Bring it on!!

I recently joined the Businesswomen Shine Online Facebook Group who are very supportive and have a great wealth of information and knowledge. Their guidance and inspiration led me to advertise more of my creations and as a result, my confidence has grown. I have amazing support from friends and family and, through my business, have met a fantastic variety of people over the years, all thanks to my love of crafting and sewing. My continuing journey to grow myself, my enterprise and my fundraising goals, will be posted on my Instagram and Facebook pages, so please feel free to follow me. Let's inspire each other.

BIO:

Teresa Barker is the creator of TheGiftShedCreations making unique cards and gifts and donates 20% of the product price to the wonderful charity, ABF The Soldiers Charity. She has been sewing and crafting for 30+ years and makes beautiful, quality products. She is very passionate about all she does and will continue to support this charity for years to come. Please feel free to follow and support her on her many social media platforms.

www.thegiftshedcreations.store

9

BECOMING A FERTILITY NUTRITIONIST AND ENTREPRENEUR

Angela Heap

After a recent ADHD diagnosis, I started to wonder if having this drive and annoying 'do or die' approach was how I have managed to successfully weather the storm of not only starting but surviving and running my own business as a fertility nutritionist when most small businesses in this area fail. In 2022 after 14 years, I manage and mentor 3 people in my clinic and am now training other nutritionists. One of the main reasons I started my own business was that I wanted to do things on my own terms. I found the politics many used to climb the career ladder really hard to play, which ultimately led me to look into what made more sense to me – and even at an early stage in my career all roads lead to being my own boss.

I'm not massively into labels but finding out at University that I had dyslexia (which has now also been layered with ADHD), gave me the opportunity to stop and take a breath and think 'I'm not a failure' (I failed my A 'levels to get to University

3 times until I got the grades) - I think differently or as the professionals say I'm Neurodiverse.

At school I was passionate about a few subjects from anthropology to environmentalism to animal welfare and even now I value and respect people who are truly passionate to a cause! The way things work in a school setting is it's a one size fits all schooling system, and in my view designed to channel people into a workforce and not an entrepreneurial approach or owning your own company.

ADHD is largely misunderstood in the UK, especially as an adult, so the way you deal with this is to push through and try and get your brain to work in the same way as others (which can reinforce feelings of failure and frustration – the "ask a fish to ride a bicycle" analogy comes up). With a poorly connected 'executive function' or prefrontal cortex that helps you with organising, timekeeping, task orientation and focus; getting from A to Z can often become insurmountable. Dopamine, the neurotransmitter in the brain that is the major player in a lot of these tasks, is often lower in people with ADHD which can mean you are often playing catch up in all the above areas or starting in deficit.

Interestingly, according to quite a lot of research, people with ADHD tend to score higher on scales measuring traits that often make people successful entrepreneurs, such as innovation, creativity and being proactive and also taking risks. The 'curse' of having this type of brain isn't all bad as seen from a mainstream perspective – it can mean there are 'superpowers' and often there are ways to tap into these areas to get to the end in a different way, or a brain super highway to creative thought processes! Another massive bonus is that often those with ADHD can hyperfocus! Give an ADHDer a career or subject they love and they will be able to immerse themselves in it fully. Or as my Mum calls it, the 'Heap obsessive gene'. And doing a bit of research on ADHD and Dyslexia was fascinating

- if you have got it it's very likely been passed down the family line.

As Steve Jobs says, you can never connect the dots going forward only backwards so looking into how I got here was definitely a pattern and connected. After studying and finally getting a degree in Sociology and Geography in 1997 and a stint working for 2 months in a BT call centre, which I hated - I embarked on a career in the charity and public sector. I loved working with people, but was never keen on the hierarchy side of things (at this stage I had no idea how this was sowing the seeds for my own business). So I started off my first job in a charity that helped people with ways to support regeneration and education in areas of deprivation; mostly in inner city and old industrial areas of the UK. I had to intern, with no pay back in the day before I got my first job officially and a salary - which was really tough for 8 months as my parents were in Germany at the time, so it was never an option to fail, so the 'ride hard or go home' approach, became 'just ride hard!!'.

This job suited me well and within a few months I had really grasped the concept of supporting and writing grant funding applications for prospective applicants and hitting more targets for them than before. It really worked out too as I was offered my first job with a charity in Manchester.

I thought I'd won the lottery getting £12k a year. After working in North West Network I travelled all over the country doing this and also worked for a few years in the local authority doing a similar job. By the time I came to London and 7 years into this sector from 2004 to 2008 at the London Voluntary sector training consortium things were beginning to wind up in the UK in regards to EU and government funding for regeneration, so I started to ask ' what next?'.

What I was doing was so niche if it ran its course there were limited things I could do – but I had a plan...during my time as an EU grants officer I'd seen a side to inequalities through my work where I saw a lot of people with diabetes and cardiovascular issues and gestational issues in pregnancy - I looked inwards to what I loved (and I looked into my interest in alternatives to improving your health through lifestyle, food and supplements). Cue a total pivot into a career as a Nutritionist.

I studied for 3 years and had no life (luckily I'd found a new hyperfocus in my interest in nutrition) and after 3 years alongside a full time job 9-5 and weekends spent at the college and clinical hours completed, I qualified in 2008. Initially I supplemented this with a few part time jobs in social enterprises inbetween to keep the cash coming in.

The early days of starting a whole new career are intense. I did cooking classes, worked in a centre for teen pregnancies, and I then worked in the team at Natural Fertility Experts as their nutritionist. I then worked to build up my contacts in well known UK health food stores and supplement companies. From 2016 I've been asked to lecture for colleges and now I'm a regular at the British College of Nutritional Health on their bachelor of science course on the subject of fertility and pregnancy. I've lectured internationally and in the UK as part of conferences to over 400 nutritionists, so I thought it was about time I started to train my own students in a new programme of my own in 2022. I also recently rebranded into AH Fertility Nutrition which suits my sense of purpose, humour and approach in the business.

I attended an event in February 2022 - the first one in a long time after covid lockdowns (something I had done regularly as part of business and networking). The evening was hosted by an Australian Probiotics company and was headed up with one of my old lecturers. Not only was it so lovely to see her, but she reminded me of how long we've known each other (since 2006) and some things that got me a bit emotional. She said 'Angela I've been watching your career and it has been remarkable, you are probably one of the most successful people from your year, the sheer determination you've shown has been amazing' one of the things I've been called before is determined (apparently it's an ADHD thing!). I quickly clapped back that she and another amazing lecturer (both now working for microbiome companies) were also my inspiration and pushed me to move into hormones and fertility. It's always worth noting that along the way to you getting your dream are people who play a pivotal part, and are quietly cheering you on as you hit every wall; mostly you smash through but many times you knock yourself out and see stars! I'd definitely not be where I am without my amazing family who always supported me emotionally to keep on pushing through especially my amazing sister.

Working to build my dream company, which is a constant remodel every year or so, is one of the proudest things in my life. My own baby that is a teenager now! It's been a long road and it's tested me to the limits (it's definitely not easy as you have to be everything and hope that your family don't get fed up with you along the way). Never switching off can take a toll and is often exhausting. Looking back sometimes it has meant going without holidays, working round the clock and borrowing a fiver or 2 from family. However as many entrepreneurs will tell you - somewhere inside there is a drive so insatiable you have to listen to it even if you are on the red petrol dial and don't know where the next paycheck will come from! If you get there and still love it, then I'd say it's worth every sleepless night, pit in stomach, rollercoaster moment. The moments when you push a button and it all works, listening and helping people to bring their own dreams into the world with starting a family is what has always kept me going. Sadly, I'm still an old softie and almost always cry when clients tell me they are pregnant!

I started my company without a business plan or loan, or a 5 year plan, although I've always had things I wanted to attain and I have always got there. It's been hard graft all the way from 2008 to now as back then social media didn't exist and the idea that diet lifestyle and functional testing could give a deeper analysis on fertility was unheard of. I'd say to anyone wanting to do this – the time is always now and it's always worth a crack. My advice is inspired by some of these amazing journeys; Don't give up, get up when you fall. Take any help you can get, and be kind to yourself. Oh and maybe invest in a mentor when the time is right to make sure you are channelling your vibe into the next level as you want to hit peak not just basecamp!

You don't know this yet but you may look back on this and marvel at how it all fell into place, as I'm a great believer in the universe guiding you gently on your way. Also authenticity and courage are what makes you the real deal so always stay true to your voice and not anyone else's, their experience has carved a different path!

BIO:

Angela Heap is the CEO of AH Fertility Nutrition; a busy Fertility Nutrition company where the team have collectively over 30 years' experience.

The clinic supports clients through tailored preconception and pregnancy programmes from 1 to 6 months. These include working with singles and couples to prepare them when they have previously had issues with fertility. Clients come from all over the world. The support given ranges from those wanting to get pregnant from various stages and through IVF and assisted methods, to egg donation and also throughout the pregnancy. The clinic also supports people through group online courses. In 2022 Angela started a mentoring programme for other nutritionists after many years of mentoring privately and being asked to teach at a variety of Colleges, conferences and events.

www.ah-fertilitynutrition.com

10

HEAL AND NOURISH TO BLOSSOM AND FLOURISH

Louise Hill

I was crouching down in the pulpit dressed all in white ready to make my appearance as Angel Gabriel in the school play, heart hammering, deep breath I stood up.

"Do not be afraid, I bring you good news and tidings of great joy……"

I finished my lines and turned my head to find my family, all I saw was their retreating backs as they left. This set a pattern for my life, be a good girl, stay in the background, you don't deserve to shine.

I was an Armed Forces child, born in Singapore and never living in one place for very long. Sent to boarding school at 9, travelling to wherever my father was posted for the school holidays. It gives you some incredible life skills. I became independent, very adaptable to change and able to empathise with many people. There is also a sense of rootlessness and a longing to come home.

Fast forward I was 35 years old laying on a couch in the Ayurvedic practitioners office with tears seeping from the corners of my eyes, later realising that she had been using Reiki, I felt such a relief as this was my wakeup call.

How had I reached this place? My mind travelled back to a while before, sitting in a similar room with the doctor announcing my test results for the helicobacter-pylori bug were off the scale, prescribing a cocktail of drugs that would kill the bacteria. I had been diagnosed with a stomach ulcer at the age of 35, my father had died of stomach cancer at the age of 63. Jay turned to me with compassion saying, your body cannot sustain you living on adrenaline all the time, you carry on like this and you will create the same circumstances that caused your fathers illness.

I had recently moved house with a four and a seven-year-old and my stress levels were off the scale, she said you have to create more balance in your life, our bodies are not designed to be in fight or flight mode (sympathetic nervous system) all the time; you have to allow your body time to rest and digest (parasympathetic nervous system). You have 2 choices, carry on like you are and develop stomach cancer or choose a different path, change your diet, attitude and life

Her first recommendation was to learn Primordial Sound Meditation with Deepak Chopra.

"Today I make the following commitments, I will not criticise, condemn or complain. Every decision I make today will be a choice between a grievance and a miracle. I am responsible for what I see, I choose the feelings I experience. I set the goals that I will achieve and let each of us ask for peace within, without and everywhere with love - Deepak".

Primordial Sound meditation involves being given a mantra which you then chant in order to stop your brain from being overactive. I was then given instructions, which I found very difficult to follow at the beginning. I even found it difficult to sit still because I was so used to rushing around all the time. Mantras are primordial sounds, the basic vibrations of nature, the wind through the trees, waves on a beach and that's why your brain responds so well to them, there was a beautiful poem that I remember and really resonated with me.

"Know that deep inside you, in the innermost recesses of your heart are the gods and goddesses of knowledge, wealth, love and compassion, nurture them and every desire that you have, will spontaneously blossom into form. The gods and goddesses only have one desire to be born"

Everything in the universe has a vibration and using ancient Vedic mathematics to identify the sound of the universe corresponding to the time and place of your birth, this is then incorporated into your mantra.

I was instructed by Jay to practice every morning and evening and slowly I managed to find the gaps in between the thoughts. I have continued to practice meditation for the last 20 years with many different teachers.

Learning meditation had such a profound effect on me because I had always been conditioned to believe that you were either right or wrong there was no grey. Meditation has only three experiences and none of them are wrong:

The first one is if you fall asleep, if you fall asleep during meditation it's not wrong, it just means that you're very tired and your body needs to recharge.

The second, which was me, is you have lots of thoughts and feel very restless and find it difficult to actually switch off. This means that you're releasing a lot of stress, so as time goes on it gets easier and easier to meditate. That's actually what helped me because the reason I got the stomach ulcer was because I was so stressed.

The final stage which doesn't happen to me very often, but occasionally, is when you are "slipping into the gap" our nervous system is calm and at peace. I call this "tuning into your intuition or talking with your soul".

The reason I found meditation so life altering , was giving myself permission to let go of any pressure or expectation as there was no right or wrong.

I also changed my diet following her recommendations and within three weeks all the symptoms had gone. I had been attending a yoga class in my local village hall and after experiencing the healing nutritional side of yoga, I chose to train with the British wheel of yoga. This was a fascinating journey incorporating meditation, asanas, oracle cards, chakras, crystals and essential oils.

It was during this journey that I started to understand synchronicity, walking into a spiritual shop one day in order to find a particular yoga book. I found the owner was very stressed and looking for a shop assistant, without thinking, my mouth opened and I said 'I can help you with that'. This ended up with me working for her a couple of days a week enabling me to learn about crystals and attending my first circle with a medium in order to learn more about spirituality.

I have not had a recurrence of the stomach ulcer and have spent the last 20 years learning how to create balance in my life, meditating every day with many different teachers.

Studying for my certificate in counselling and having counselling myself, helped me to understand my learnt behaviours and triggers. I choose to release all that didn't benefit me. Style Coaching enabled me to combine all my skills, helping ladies feel good, look good, assessing their body shape, style personality and colour palette. Decluttering their wardrobe and then planning a shopping trip.

It was the decluttering part of my job as a Style Coach that I enjoyed the most. Letting go of all the clothes that no longer suit you, actually helps create and bring new energy into your life, you need to be ruthless when sorting out your closet and honest with yourself about what you would like to wear again. If you haven't worn something for more than a year it is a good sign that you either need to pass it onto someone who will give it to a charity or sell it. Anything permanently stained, bobbled and marks that won't come out, is best off in the recycling bin. Hanging clothes in an orderly way is the secret to making the most of your own wardrobe, it helps you see at a glance what outfits you can put together. Hanging items up allows air to circulate through the fibres keeping them fresh like opening all the windows in your house when spring comes. I then chose to do another course 'Clear your Clutter' with Feng Shui to be able declutter all aspects of my life.

During that time another synchronicity occurred when I was catching the train to see a friend in London and ended up sitting next to a lady that used to come into the Spiritual shop that I worked in a few years before. We got chatting and realised that spirit was encouraging us to set up a Spiritual Group in Winchester, which we then ran for a few years until she moved to France.

Our journey is always evolving, I entered the menopause a year ago which is an interesting journey involving hot sweats and barely any sleep! This coincided with an empty nest and the pandemic. I had space to try something new. I started attending the "Journey of the heart" circles, the sense of connection and community was exactly what I needed after feeling isolated and scattered with all the uncertainty.

Held by the inspiring Gemma from 'Sister Stories' whose mission is to make attending women's circles as common as going to yoga class.

I have chosen to retrain and run women's circles. I hold women's circles in person at 2 beautiful locations in central Winchester, UK and also via Zoom.

. . .

BIO:

Louise has played many roles during her 55 years on this planet - daughter, sister, mother friend, personnel officer, yoga teacher, Style Coach, seeker of sacred truth and angel mystic, none of which have defined her as she is ever evolving. Spending the last 20 years healing her roots, finding what nourishes her soul, she is now ready to embrace her wise women (Fu*k it fifties) stage and Flourish …..!

www.rosesandroots.co.uk

11

FROM ORDINARY TO EXTRAORDINARY

Monika Zampa

E very morning he would come downstairs and ask me: "Hey babe, what's for breakfast?"

This simple sentence would drive me mad; I mean "insanely" mad.

An avalanche of deep triggers would explode like a hot lava.

This simple phrase would immediately bring me back to my roots. Seeing my Czech grandmother slaving away in the kitchen for her sons and a tyrannical husband.

She gave birth to 5 boys...

One of them was my dad.

I used to visit her during summers. Sadly, not frequently enough.

Her life went through scrubbing the floors on her knees, cooking and providing for the family.

Cooking and cleaning, cleaning and cooking

Looking after the whole family, whilst her efforts went unnoticed.

When she died at 88, only a handful of people attended her funeral.

That Was My Grandmother

I always remember her, as a woman of service.

Service to her family. Not being respected by anybody, especially her husband.

She gave her life, her dreams and talents, her body and her future to be a great mum and great wife.

For a long time, I believed that my ultimate drive for building an online business, with the aim of becoming financially free, was, in fact, for my 9-year-old daughter.

But actually, what I am doing is expanding my capacity to RECEIVE, HOLD and MULTIPLY my money for her, and for all "forgotten" grandmothers.

To honour their lives.

To honour all the lives of other women who gave themselves in (home) service.

To honour all women around the world who are still hiding, keeping small, and being silent.

Back to my story

This simple sentence would bring all of these feelings back. When I would explain this to my boyfriend at the time, politely asking him NOT to greet me in THAT manner, because it triggered pain in me, he would repeat it the next day and all the days thereafter.

Toxic relationships are like a mosaic of seemingly insignificant daily stories, when compounded over time, they had escalated with the expression of that one phrase.

Fast forward 11 years

Today, I am a business owner with a coaching and energy healing business who is using public speaking to spread my message and grow my business fast.

I have become an expert at rebuilding women's self-confidence and courage. I solve 3 major problems, many powerful business women secretly face these days:

1. the destructive inner voice
2. keeping herself small so others can shine
3. undervaluing her talents

I help ambitious women to RISE from toxic relationships by stopping the negative self-talk so they can EXPAND their capacity to claim, allow and RECEIVE ABUNDANCE and create financial freedom for themselves.

The tools I confidently recommend to my clients are highly effective, with long lasting effect, practical and easy to implement. And most of all, tried and tested on myself.

"My business is the journey I had to take, the lessons I had to learn and overcome, so I could evolve into the confident woman I am today."

I have transformed my limiting beliefs about money and codependency. Freed myself from stories which were holding me and my feminine karmic lineage for decades. Filled my cup of self love to the ULTIMATE high and an overflow.

I now pass this gift of transformation to others.

Life is a kaleidoscopic picture of all the ups and downs, challenges and wins. Often with moments of desperation, where you find yourself on your knees, gazing at the vast sky, eyes wide open and asking, begging the "Higher Powers" to help you.

If I had to put my life on a measuring scale I would say that for 80% of my life I have been happy, joyous, fun filled and beautiful. I see beauty and gratitude in everything, in all situations.

A tiny flower courageously blossoming on the spring branch will ignite joy and gratitude in my heart for days.

Life is picturesque and full of adventures. And we get to CHOOSE.

I will never forget the moment, when as a young ex-investment banker in the City of London, after quitting my banking job on moral grounds, I stepped into the most humid, pungently smelling hustle of humanity outside Delhi Airport grounds.

Before I left London, my colleagues would enviously and in disbelief see me quit, decline a pay- rise and sell all my belongings and follow my dreams.

I took one year off to explore and travel the world. With the aim of "finding myself" after an emotionally draining divorce.

In search of "enlightenment" I followed a Buddhist path into places, where Buddha was born (Lumbini), attained enlightenment (Bodghaya under Bodhi tree) and where he had died (Kushinagara).

It was supposed to be one year off, with a possibility of returning back to the banking career... it never, thankfully, happened and because of a new romance, I ended up in Amsterdam, where I still reside now, until my next intended destination, Ibiza, Spain.

Little did I know that India is a place you either love or hate. Like Marmite, no discussion about it. I loooooove Marmite with corn crackers and butter. And I totally fell in love with India too. [it took some adjusting for a conditioned City Banker Brain].

Work smarter not harder. More free time, more fun!

My mum and sisters fully support my entrepreneurial journey. Paradoxically, I still secretly deep inside would like my dad to say: "well done, I am proud of you".

It takes tremendous courage and self-knowledge to admit this. I feel proud to share this with you, fully knowing that there are women reading this and saying: "Yes, yes, me too!"

According to Freud, we begin to have an animosity toward the same-sex parent when we are young, because we develop a sexual attraction to the parent of the opposite sex.

Well, I am not totally sure about this, but what rings a bell is that a father (or a male caregiver) is the first male a young girl creates a relationship with. He inevitably becomes her ideal future male (mate) model. She creates a bond for life and sculpts (subconsciously) all her future "significant others" on her father's characteristics. The good ones and the bad ones.

Never getting the approval of my father is the first struggle I had to overcome. And overcome, I did, at the age 45+ by practising Ho'oponopono, the Hawaiian prayer, which formed an integral part of my Body Therapist study.

My teacher, Amira, would drill into me, we first need to clear the "canoe" in order for us to connect with our purpose and mission in life and reach our goals.

The canoe will not float in the vast ocean and reach the desired destination, if we do not deal with any unresolved issues in our ancestral paths. Starting with Mother and Father figures. Finding the courage to initiate weekly phone calls, write letters, messages is the path to take.

It took me one year to build a bulletproof shell around my being and restart the communication with my father. And, by doing so, a massive burden dropped away, creating more light in my life. Attracting beautiful and soulful like-minded people into my life.

I invite you to ask yourself, where is your canoe going? Do you have a destination you want to reach?

The hunger for freedom of choice and expression, seeing women safely voicing their needs, being heard and noticed, without a fear of being criticised, ridiculed, laughed at or totally dismissed. This holds my values and visions really high and helps me to stay on course.

My second massive WHY is women becoming financially abundant, so they can act from DESIRE and not from must, from CHOICE and not from need.

As far as I can remember, I always felt the burden of women suffering in the world. I did not know how to explain it and never told anybody about this. It felt like I was connected with them through an invisible light matrix. The women who suffered, the female circumcision, sexual workers, the abused ones and the silenced ones.

I was about 15 years old growing up in Prague, surrounded by grey high rise cement block buildings [we were lucky as our building was "cute" 3 floor high]. I remember leaning out of my bedroom window, on one hot summer night and sneakily listening to the unusual sounds.

A Roma family with 10 kids were living in the opposite high-rise block. The sounds intrigued me. It was a mixture of singing, kids screaming, shouting, making love and probably some domestic violence. I was addicted to the wildness. Feeling ashamed that it aroused some sexual feelings within me. I have put a tight lid on it.

Now, I know that sexual energy is pure and unstoppable. It is LIFE energy! Without it nothing will grow and prosper. Those hidden moments aroused my zest for freedom.

I secretly admired the "out of norm" families, for being rebels.

It took me about 25 years to realise and fully celebrate my

rebel, outspoken, out of the box, different, odd one out, being. I am no square peg, being forced into a round hole.

The ability to connect deeply on the heart's level, to be able to see my clients for WHO they truly are, dropping the masks of mother, sister, daughter, CEO, corporate leader and hold a space for them to release and open up within a safe environment, free from judgement, criticism and pressure.... This is my gift to the world.

My purpose and mission in life is simple. To share my life's journey and the extraordinary transformation with other women, so they get inspired to take action and rise from toxic environments and expand the capacity to DESERVE, ALLOW and RECEIVE ABUNDANCE.

Behind every female entrepreneur is a businesswoman, with a desire to create an impact in the world. This impact comes from a deep knowing.

If not NOW then WHEN
     If not ME then WHO

BIO:

Monika is an internationally renowned keynote Public Speaker, Empowerment Coach and Energy Healer for Women.

Originally a Czech/Russian, currently living in Amsterdam, proud mother of a beautiful daughter.

An ex-investment banker from City of London, left on moral grounds, travelled around the world, embarked on a 25+ year journey of self-discovery and healing

In recent years walking the entrepreneurial path towards financial independence.

Energy healings, family constellation, mindset reprogramming, empowerment coaching. All these are delivered in a 3 step Rapid Transformational Process called The Diamond Method.

Monika effectively mentors powerful career women to rise from toxic relationships by stopping the negative inner chit chat and expanding the capacity to allow, claim and receive ABUNDANCE

www.monikazampa.com

12

CONCEPTION OF AN IDEA

Kate Adey

I n my twenties, I unknowingly had an intuitive sense of the work I wanted to do, and when to move on from a job that didn't sit well with me. I also questioned whether I wanted to conform to the traditional career path that I could see so many around me were taking.

I can now see that my approach naturally led me to having clarity and confidence, and to knowing what next step to take. Back then, I didn't realise that my ease and flow in choosing to move careers was what I would end up exploring at a deeper level.

In January 2007, I had our first baby boy. I was on maternity leave from the consulting firm and was doing a Masters in Management Learning and Leadership at Lancaster University. It was then that I acknowledged the feeling that it might be time to set up my own business. The learning space, amazingly supportive tutor and tutor group gave me the chance to reflect, to be challenged and to explore what my business might be.

Having spent nearly 15 years in corporate consulting, firstly for a very large global firm and then for a much smaller company, I saw that what I loved in the work I did was the coaching element. Looking back now, what I was also doing was a lot of questioning to find out the source of the leadership models we were using with clients. There were hundreds of different models and hundreds more could be created. I wanted to know something deeper that underpinned these models of thinking.

This was a key reason for me wanting to start my business, so that I could go deeper into understanding the nature of our being and bring that into the corporate work I loved doing. What I didn't know then was my Masters dissertation would become a big part of the coaching work I was to go on and do.

I can remember a very emotional moment when I realised, I wanted my dissertation to be the voice of women returning to corporate life after maternity leave and explore how to let organisations know their challenges and what support they would need during this important transition. I was also experiencing this myself, which made it feel even more special.

I returned to the small consulting firm after nine-months leave, with the feeling of it being the time to do my own thing still very much present. However, in January 2008, I found I was pregnant with our second baby! This was 'a holy cow' moment. It couldn't have come at a worse time. How would I set up my coaching business now? I would have to delay it.

Thankfully, my intuition kicked in and I knew I needed to follow the feeling of joy, excitement, and possibility instead of fear for the future. I set up Kate Adey Coaching in May 2008, pregnant for the second time and part way through my Masters. My ego was telling me I was crazy, however I knew it was the right next step for me.

Going it alone... or so I thought

Networking was something I enjoyed doing and through this received some coaching work with an old client for my first year as Kate Adey Coaching. However, I knew I wanted to do maternity transition coaching, using the work from my dissertation and my own experience. I began sharing this ambition for my business with close friends and I was introduced to a magic circle law firm. After several meetings they asked me to pitch for the maternity coaching contract. I was overjoyed and surprised – they'd asked me!

I wanted to collaborate on the pitch, so again I contacted everyone I knew and asked for recommendations. I was introduced to a wonderful lady and although we didn't win that contract, we did well. However, I did not stop there and reached out to the law firm to ask who did win. If you never ask, you never know! I found out who won and was drawn to contacting them. It was My Family Care and on meeting the head of consulting and coaching; we hit it off. She welcomed me to work with them as an Associate Coach and suggested the law firm be my first client. I was thrilled and have been working with My Family Care for eleven years.

This was a great opportunity to do the work I loved and be part of a learning community. The work I did through My Family Care grew and at the same time, so did our family. We had our third boy in 2012 whilst transitioning onto my third maternity leave, I used the opportunity to do some deeper work - questioning what was really going on in life, with me and with my clients.

I became really interested in understanding what it means to be a human being and spent many a moment going within and finding the answers for myself. This was aided by reading books, about leadership, psychology, the brain, mind, and spirituality. A key book that changed my thinking was 'The Missing Link' by Sydney Banks. I realised I had been focussing my attention on all the activities, thoughts, feelings, perceptions of my experience instead of noticing what is always there and that doesn't come and go.

Knowing I was onto something I continued my investigation into the nature of our being, what's happening when we are in flow, by getting into conversation with those who were ahead of me in their exploration. I joined groups run by Garret Kramer, attended seminars, and continued to read and listen to teachers such as Rupert Spira, Michael Neill and Rhonda Burns (The Greatest Secret).

This was very much a non-rational exploration and refined my way of seeing myself, others, and reality. I was having regular realisations that who I am is more than my psychology, that I am what is constant and continuous not what is transitory – call that Awareness, Being, Love, Joy, Peace, Consciousness or God. I also saw that everyone and everything share this being – we are a shared being.

What I have found isn't anything new. It's not something we need to gain or learn. It's a stripping away of this understanding in ourselves as being a separate entity (mind and body) and sinking back into the knowing that has never left us.

Heading into the future with confidence and excitement

I am now in a place where my coaching business has three focus areas.

One is supporting parents with their parental transition in a practical and profound way. I really enjoy being part of an Associate coaching team at My Family Care (now Bright Horizons), dedicated to serving large corporate clients with pre, during, and on return specialist coaching.

The second area focuses on working directly with corporates to support all parents in their return to work. We design a bespoke practice that contributes to creating a nurturing and supportive culture. This includes focused coaching sessions with career/performance development partners and virtual group coaching for cohorts of parents across different business areas, which brings a networking and supportive element to the work. I am working with organisations committed to supporting their people to make the right life and work choices. I love creating the space for exploration of the nature of self and realisations to take place. Magic happens!

Finally, I am a Quality of Mind (QoM) Coach which is leadership coaching and team development that explores 'before psychology'. This business opportunity came about when I heard Piers Thurston, founder of Quality of Mind, interviewing Rupert Spira (author and non-duality teacher). What Piers was saying and pointing to really resonated so I got in touch. We had a long chat as we walked across fields and discovered that we had taken very similar paths.

I had the pleasure of attending a three-day QoM Open Programme, run by Piers, which reinforced the immense value of pointing clients to what lies behind all experience. Or to put another way, what comes before our psychology. I am excited to be working with and mentored by Piers, and to bring my own clients to the table as I step into this work in the corporate world. Appearing as a guest on his QoM Podcast to discuss 'Is there really no such thing as a difficult relationship in the business world?' was a great experience.

For me QoM underpins all the coaching and work I do, be that with leadership teams or parents returning to work after leave. It's the essence of who I am, and my mission is to continue to find ways to bring this understanding to people in business.

I've struggled in the past to define my coaching and now can clearly say that QoM is at the cutting edge of where organisations and its people need to go to find peak performance and productivity, the source of relationships and wellbeing, and lasting inner peace and happiness.

Who knows what the future holds. I would love to be doing more QoM work with leaders and their teams and would like to reach many more parents in the corporate world to support them in their transitions. I'd also love to appear on some radio shows, do more podcasts, and create a community for returners where learning, practical tips and profound realisations can take place.

BIO:

Kate is a highly regarded leadership and transformation coach specialising in leadership, performance, and parent transition coaching. Kate draws on over 20 years of consulting experience in high-pressure environments, to support the leaders she now works with. Since qualifying as a coach in 2003 Kate has navigated her own transitions and has completed Academic-based research on transitioning to motherhood and returning to work. Kate coaches returning parents to access the clarity and wisdom they need to reintegrate successfully, and confidently take the next career move.

Through deep self-inquiry Kate has evolved her own coaching practice and brings a depth to her work which is routed in the principles behind Quality of mind (QoM) which works upstream to the mind; before psychology, making her work with leaders truly transformative.

Kate is married to James and is a mother to three boys. She lives in Somerset, loves to do all year-round open water swimming, run with the family black lab, and cook healthy family meals.

www.kateadey.co.uk

13

WELL, WHAT ARE THE CHANCES?

Gemma Willsher

I f you'd told me 20 years ago as I sat staring at 6 screens on the trading floor of a US investment bank that today I'd be describing how I came to co-own and run a private medical practice, I'd have put the chances at a billion to one. But then again, I have always subscribed to a pin-ball machine analogy of life. You don't always have to know exactly where you're going, just keep moving, and when you hit something, you're sure to bounce off at an intriguing angle.

Life dealt me an excellent opening hand. My parents were loving, clever and hard working. Both of them are shining examples of the social mobility afforded by the grammar school system, which took them from very humble working class back-grounds to being the first graduates in their families. And because of their humble beginnings, they watched every single penny; not in a stingy way, but to make sure that all the money earned was channelled towards what they felt was really important. For them, this was education for my brother and me.

In Norfolk, where we lived, the grammar school system had been replaced with comprehensives. My father, a teacher, had done some supply work in our catchment school and didn't like what he saw. So they decided we would 'go private'. This was no small undertaking on teachers' salaries (it wouldn't be even remotely possible today).

While my school friends went on skiing holidays and to DisneyLand – we made an annual pilgrimage to stay in a static caravan in the northernmost reaches of the Scottish highlands. It took forever to drive there, but the location was idyllic on the shore of a loch looking out at the Isle of Skye. The weather was frequently atrocious, so on the days stuck inside, I was taught Bridge by the octogenarian retired university lecturer who rented us the caravan. During one particularly poor week of weather, I remember casually asking what the chances were of shuffling the cards in to suit order.

"That would be *one in 52 factorial*", replied my Dad (maths and science definitely his thing).

This was his explanation: 52x51x50x49... and so on all the way down to x1. It was odd to the 12-year-old me that the world hadn't come up with the actual number yet – this was the 1980s after all. Sadly I didn't have access to the cutting edge home computer of the day, a ZX Spectrum, but undeterred and supremely confident in my long multiplication skills, I set about to remedy the situation using pen and paper.

I will save you the nail biting suspense of googling – the answer is 8.0658175e+67, or you may prefer 'about 80 *unvigintillion*' (Yes, that is a thing). But the main point for the purposes of this story, is that it's a number that has *68* zeros... And thus having plodded down as far as x45 (answer for those playing along at home, 3.0342338e+13) I ran out of paper and had my earliest lesson in the wisdom of scoping a project before committing to it.

Factorial calculations aside, I jumped through the academic hoops with relative ease, helped in no small part by my school being all girls – particularly important, I believe, for confidence in maths and science subjects. Public exams passed with a pleasing slew of A grades, and being a 'bit of a talker', I ended up eschewing numbers temporarily in favour of a Modern Languages degree at Oxford. In the penultimate year of my degree, my inner maths nerd returned as I contemplated graduate starting salaries, and after comparing them with one bedroom rents in London, I fired off applications to all the major investment banks. Eventually I was accepted.

The City

My career made a heady start with 10 weeks spent in a condominium on the upper West Side of New York. As a graduate cohort we practised Excel modelling by day, used our English accents to blag our way into nightclubs by night, and got up at 5am to go to the gym before our next assessment.

Once back in London, I assumed my position in a cubicle on the 5th floor of an enormous corporate 'death star' on Victoria Embankment as an 'analyst'. This meant I did spreadsheets – lots of them – and then tried to sound convincing about the numbers they spat out when anyone asked. The working day was long and brutal – the London market opened at 7am and I was at my desk at 06:45, and frequently still there past 9pm. Daylight was a stranger to me between October and March. Days passed in an adrenaline-and-caffeine-fuelled-blur of quick fire and expletive strewn exchanges with our trading floor.

In terms of the business culture, the bonus grail drove everyone's behaviour – it was a paranoid and dog-eat-dog world, and when on 'letter day' you found out your number, the thrill was quickly replaced with distrust and paranoia if you had even the slightest inkling that others had got more.

Looking back, I know now that I was burned out, but putting on a brave face. Initially I blamed the Pill for feeling crappy, as, when I accidentally came off it on holiday, I felt like a huge weight had been lifted from my shoulders. But this clearly masked other underlying issues, as 2 years later, my periods still hadn't returned. I tried acupuncture, hypnotherapy, and ultimately went to the onsite private GP at work. He assured me confidently that 'switching my periods back on' would be as simple as taking some clomiphene, and I left his office with a prescription in hand.

Several months later, I had gained an unexpected familiarity with the smooth follicle-free outline of my ovaries on ultrasound. They were, apparently, perfectly healthy, but in stasis – sulking almost, impervious to any chemical stimuli. My gynae eventually threw in the towel and said, "time to get out the big guns" (or words to that effect), and I was referred to a fertility clinic for hormone injections.

As she dictated my referral letter in front of me, my gynaecologist noted *en passant* 'you probably have one of those silly jobs in the City where you work *all hours God sends'*... funny she should mention ... And so, as if by some divine intervention, it came to pass mere months later that in one of the periodic rounds of redundancies that cycle through the City in sync with the FTSE graph, my number came up. The sense of relief was palpable.

New life

And so began my new life, which consisted pretty exclusively of trying to get pregnant, and in the least sexy or romantic way possible. I thought fertility clinics were for people with old eggs, or not enough eggs. I was under 30, with no significant physical markers of ill health. Surely going to a fertility clinic just to get an egg out was like using a sledge-hammer to crack a nut? But then this is the girl who tried to calculate 52 factorial. In the initial consultation, the potential cost of each fertility cycle was starting to hit home. I found myself, not for the first time, staring despondently at a very large number of zeros. The consultant saw me weaken and threw in that he would also recommend a comprehensive panel of auto-immune blood tests, approximate cost £80 *unvigintillion* 'just in case'.

"This can help us know what to do if you have repeated miscarriages once you get pregnant."

I pondered the calculation, and my track record to date.

"Shall we just get an egg out first, and see where that takes us?"

Incredibly fortunately our first full cycle of IVF was success-ful, and my daughter arrived in 2006, followed in 2009 by boy/girl twins, also IVF. With 3 children under the age of three, I fell into what I now call 'the blip' – a sleep deprived period of 18 months during which my knowledge of 'the world at large' centred around who read the CBeebies bedtime story. The banking crisis, birth of Twitter, Instagram, and The Arctic Monkeys, to name but the smallest selection, all fully passed me by.

Still, as time went by, tiny pockets of breathing space started to appear, and I turned my mind to the next big project. Having stopped paid work before I even conceived, I was feeling professionally rudderless, except for knowing unequivocally that I would never put myself through the City again. As a first step, I decided to re-train as a clinical hypnotherapist, and on qualifying started a small practice in Covent Garden. My clien-tele was heavily populated with ex-colleagues and their peers, all of whom proved a sad indictment of the kind of burn out I had experienced.

In 2013 our family beat the well-worn path out of southwest London to re-settle in Hampshire. Within a few months, my youngest started reception, and I had a few hallowed hours (between 10am and 2pm) to contemplate my next move! I temped happily for a while, and also interviewed for some permanent roles but felt the significant headwind of explaining my 'surprisingly long' career break. If I'm honest, when I contemplated the logistical (not to mention emotional) back flips that would be inherent in selling my time to an employer, I very quickly lost heart.

Around this time, I was approached by a GP friend who, having recently become a Partner at a Hampshire GP practice, was rapidly becoming disillusioned. Much as the 'free at point of delivery' ideal sounds so right in principle, the 'on the ground' reality was dominated by frustration, both for patients (wait times) and practitioners (who were prevented by budgets and processes from offering the best possible care to individual patients). Something had to change.

Finding fulfilment

We had nothing but raw enthusiasm, and a very clear idea of what amazing care ought to look like to start us off. I was delighted to be able to utilise the skills I sharpened in the corporate world, but now as a seasoned user of healthcare, not to mention a mother, it felt incredible to be putting my skills to use in a way that could genuinely improve people's lives.

Obviously, I had never run a GP practice and had no idea what it involved, so I logged onto the CQC website (our regulator) to get my first taste. "Hoorah!", I thought, "These guys keep things simple" – there are 'only' 5 lines of enquiry, whether the service is: Safe, Caring, Effective, Responsive and Well Led. This is, I can now confirm, the medical management's version of calculating 52 factorial, except with constantly shifting parameters, not least when a virus came along some time in 2019 to turn everyone's world upside down.

We saw our first patient in October 2015 and have been happily and consistently growing ever since. I'm proud to say now that I come to work not just to support my family, but also to enjoy myself while hanging out with a team of the very best humans. I have a genuine sense of purpose and fulfilment. Winchester GP may never 'scale' in a corporate sense. If it does, it won't be at the expense of our mission to provide the kind of care that we'd want for our own nearest and dearest. We'll also be ever mindful of the significant sacrifices many people make to access private care.

When will I have finished scoping this project? It's impossible to say, but if I ever claim that I have, please tell me to go back and check my workings!

BIO:

Gemma Willsher is the Co-Founder and Practice Manager for Winchester GP, offering superlative private GP services throughout Hampshire.

www.winchestergp.com

SAGEING GRACEFULLY

Margaret Barrie

P ushing envelopes makes for an eventful life.

Born the only girl in a large family, I grew up being told that "girls couldn't….shouldn't…mustn't…." Outwardly I was submissive; internally I shaped my own quiet way of defying the dictates of my brothers and often the world. I had the unwitting support of a father who insisted that I should be well-educated and musical, should be my mother's support in all things domestic and should never argue with or question authority. Well – not openly!

Moving forward some decades, retirement had little appeal. After many adventures, travels and discoveries, a long-held dream of mine was finally possible. I moved to the UK. Prior to departing South Africa (my place of birth), I had become an internationally accredited Gallup Strengthsfinder® coach, having decided that my time consulting as a counselling psychologist had reached a good endpoint. I needed a more positive approach to assisting people to manage and master the challenges of their personal and professional lives. On landing in the UK, I soon realised that the best option was to create my own coaching business and thus started my solopreneur adventure. Trusting my internal grit, supported by two entrepreneurial daughters and many other inspiring and encouraging women (and men!), I had many guides and mentors so set forth with clarity of purpose.

And then, less than a year after I'd landed in the UK, COVID! Now, almost three years later, uncertainty continues in many aspects of life. However, it's a case of onward and upward! No matter the obstacles, my purpose is to build a coaching practice that makes a positive difference in people's lives so they, in turn, can make a difference in the lives of others.

To set the scene for the current role I play, perhaps I may share some of the high points of my life. At 14, I was privileged to spend a couple of years in Dublin where I attended a fabulous school and experienced an independence not available to a young girl growing up in South Africa, where, even in the early 1950s, it was not "safe" to be out and about alone. On returning to South Africa to complete schooling, the comparative restrictions became like a straightjacket and were the source of much frustration. However, as learnt early in life, when one door closes, look for and open another. I could choose to be frustrated by the limitations or find something new on which to focus my attention. Fortune smiled on me by bringing a new teacher to the school who was a specialist in Afrikaans – at the time, this was the second official language in the country. I had six months in which to master the language sufficiently to pass my final exams. She made this possible and was a great inspiration.

University in a different city was the next challenge – women were very much the minority on campus, especially in the sciences which I was studying – dietetics and nutrition to be exact. Somehow, I muddled through (in Afrikaans) to qualify, by which time I had married. I worked as a dietitian in a major hospital for a couple of years and then family life took over. Because I have a somewhat insatiable thirst for knowledge and experiences, life was full of adventures and changes. We spent a few years in the UK, returned to South Africa, moved to Zimbabwe, back to South Africa – you have the picture!

As it was important for me to be a very present parent for our two daughters, I took on any sort of part-time work that interested me and did not interfere with my parenting. One of the more random things I did was to run the office at a horse-riding facility. A major international horse show was planned and I was swept into doing the PR and helping to mount a highly exciting and entertaining pageant based on mediaeval jousting. We had enormous fun inventing ways to create "chain-mail" – if you need to know how, please request the pattern and my way of making string look like armour!

Probably the most gratifying of all the "other" sort of work I did, was being invited to teach school music at a newly opened secondary school in Zimbabwe. Apart from what I had to learn (often one small leap ahead of my pupils!), the stimulating company of the rest of the staff and the variety of new pursuits in which to get involved, were an ongoing source of fascination. I also had the great joy of having both my daughters join the school and become very involved with all that was on offer. That came to an end when we moved back to South Africa. Once the dust of that move had settled, I started my own private practice as a consultant dietitian, at the same time studying an Arts honours degree, taking my time as it needed to be fitted in amongst so many other things.

The next big adventure came once the girls had flown the nest. I packed myself up and moved to Seattle, USA for a couple of years where I studied a Masters in counselling psychology. Yet another rich learning experience.

On returning once again to South Africa, I established a private practice and worked as a psychologist for the best part of twenty five years, until I finally realised my dream of moving to the UK.

In sum, my route to solopreneurship has been long and varied, often daunting though always stimulating and challenging. The people I have met along the way came from all walks of life; from each I learnt. And all the threads of learning have woven together to form the backcloth to the current role I play as a coach, counsellor and mentor.

People fascinate me and it is such a joy to be invited into the labyrinth of thinking, feeling and experiencing of another's life; to be entrusted with others' stories and vulnerabilities and then coach them to choose new ways of being with greater awareness and sensitivity to their wisest course of action.

From a business perspective, it's been a really steep learning curve, not least in regard to marketing. In the medical professions, marketing oneself was seen as unethical and unprofessional – one built a practice by referral and word of mouth. While this is equally true in business, letting the world know about one's service, experience and expertise is crucial. I needed to come to terms with talking about myself in what initially felt like a bragging or boastful way. The spectre of all those brothers, asking me who I thought I was, loomed large whenever I wanted to put my new business out into the world. In order to let go of those doubts, it was helpful to remember that, in adulthood, my brothers became the greatest and best of cheerleaders. Knowing how important it is to be heard in the noisy online world, it was a good decision to find and employ a champion in the form of someone whose expertise was marketing in social media. Whilst I use technology to the best of my ability, it's not something that comes naturally to me and it's often a step over which I fall.

One of the best things (post COVID) happened when my

daughter and a business partner built an amazing online business community for solopreneurs who have all been generous with help, support and guidance. One of the major challenges of COVID for owner-run businesses has been the isolation and lack of readily available support. This network proved to be a gamechanger, especially as technology has evolved that allows for an online co-working space – and I have finally got my head around using it!!

My business has evolved, as have my business goals and how I deliver coaching. However, the nature of what I do is still rooted in positive psychology, in particular the way Gallup® have used its theory to focus attention and development on people's natural gifts and talents. This is of particular value in a world that more and more recognises that "difference" is not a limitation so much as a unique way of being human. It is this very aspect of coaching that draws me so strongly to the profession. It is incredibly gratifying to see the shift in someone when there's a deepened understanding and acceptance of personal potential which, once acknowledged, can be developed and matured to best performance. This understanding and acceptance is multiplied when the principles are applied in coaching teams.

BIO:

Margaret Barrie is a Gallup Strengthsfinder® coach. She has a BSc in Dietetics and an MA in counselling psychology; and an ongoing need to learn and develop. Her latest area of exploration (though not formally) is neuroscience, understanding the way the brain operates and how best to enhance performance. Her major hobbies are music and the arts, hiking and travelling.

www.margaretbarrie.com

15

CREATING HARMONY IN BUSINESS

Emma Baylin

I always knew I wanted to sing. I sang everywhere. Not just in private but walking down the street, on the train, I couldn't stop. When I sang, I would become totally absorbed in the experience, the song filled my heart and my soul, making me feel complete and happy. I wanted to sing every day and my dream was to be a star in musicals.

But I was surrounded by messages that led me to believe that becoming a singer was not something a girl from a small, working-class town in the North could achieve, so common sense and a need to train for a 'real career' won out over my pleas to be sent to stage school.

Instead I followed my second passion – People. I would 'people watch' with my mum if we were waiting in the car or sitting in a café. I was intrigued by human behaviour. I also had a desire to help. I had an abundance of love and care that needed an outlet. At age 15 I took a course and position as a peer counsellor in my school and from there followed volunteering and finally a career in youth and community work.

Little did I know back then, that years later, I would combine this with my passion for singing to realise my life's purpose through my own company Shared Harmonies CIC.

I first had the inspiration for Shared Harmonies in around 2009 but I didn't register the company until October 2013. My career had developed in me a driving passion to create a sense of community and to help people feel happier and healthier. My ambition was to achieve that through singing.

Although I knew what I wanted in terms of outcomes for my participants, I couldn't clearly form the shape of the company in my mind and I was very aware that I knew nothing about running a business. I knew I wanted to reach as many people as possible and I didn't want financial circumstances to prevent people from participating.

I was successful in getting a place on the School for Social Entrepreneurs (SSE) start up programme. It was here, that as well as consolidating my thinking around the practicalities of my business, that I had my first big learning.

Find your tribe

Being a sole entrepreneur can be a lonely journey. Having others to talk to, who are on their own but comparable journey, can be the thing that helps you keep going on a bad day. Don't forget to celebrate the wins too, yours and theirs!!

While supported by the SSE, I clarified my aim for Shared Harmonies, values and my target audience. I had initially intended to work solely in communities, focussing on people with long term health and wellbeing conditions but I realised I had a great offer for workplaces too. I registered Shared Harmonies as a Community Interest Company (CIC) enabling the company to make a profit in one area (workplace wellbeing) and reinvest that to support the community side of the business.

I also realised how important my values are to me and that they were a large part of what was driving my ambitions for Shared Harmonies. I have come back to my company values many times as Shared Harmonies has developed, when designing services, when choosing my team, and most recently to help me keep going when the pandemic hit.

Values

Be clear on your organisational values. They help to give you focus and inform decision making. They can help your customers connect with you and as the company grows, they can help your team bond around a shared sense of purpose.

Since that first SSE programme, I have also been on their scale up programme and received business development support through The Growth Hub, Entrepreneurial Spark and NatWest. There are lots of these programmes around and I highly recommend applying. I am still connected to people I met through them, who are a constant source of encouragement and support. When you start your own business it is often from one passion but suddenly you have to be an accountant, a marketer, a sales person and much more. I'm so grateful to have people and programmes who have helped me with this.

Ask for help

There will be moments when you feel stuck. Being an entrepreneur is a constant learning journey. I guarantee there is no single business owner who has not needed advice, help or support in one way or another multiple times. You'll be amazed at how many people are willing to offer help.

However, asking for help is only one side of the coin, giving back is also important and I've experienced it and it has often helped me in some unexpected ways. Even though I always have more to learn myself, I have found many ways in which my support has been useful to others.

Give back

Think about ways you can support others. Be a listening ear, connect people, share your influence, your story or your expertise. You could also consider your social value, giving a percentage of profits to a community or charitable cause or offering them a free service.

From the start of my entrepreneurial journey I felt both simultaneously right where I was meant to be and completely out of my depth. I knew Shared Harmonies was my soul's purpose but I had no idea how to make it a successful business. I looked for and seized every opportunity for development, connections or broadening my awareness, whether that be a course, a conversation, networking or delivery opportunity. Many times I was completely out of my comfort zone. This was my first time running a business with many 'firsts' along the way. I reflect constantly and take the learning from each experience good and bad.

My first big opportunity was presented immediately after my interview for the first SSE programme. A member of the panel worked for a large corporate, liked my pitch and invited me to deliver a team building workshop. I felt completely unprepared. I believed in my idea but had never delivered my corporate workshop before. I did it, gaining my first glowing testimonial and gaining in confidence. 8 years on, it still brings me so much joy to see the incredible transformational journey of participants and organisations when I get them singing together.

My second opportunity, came from an old contact asking

me to deliver as part of an existing leadership programme. That experience led to the development of a new service and to us securing more 'big name' clients. Our leadership sessions are now one of our most highly rated services.

I have had to get comfortable with taking risks as an entrepreneur , especially as my company has grown. Not all risks have paid off, but when they haven't, there has always been some learning I could take from the experience. Every business owner has made many mistakes, but I have found that if I learn, adapt and move forward, each 'mistake' has left me stronger than before. If you calculate risks, you can put things in place where possible to mitigate against negative impacts.

Seize Opportunities and Take Risks

Put yourself out there and make the most of every opportunity. Get used to getting out of your comfort zone. This is where you will realise your biggest opportunities and learn your biggest lessons. Learn from every mistake - you are bound to make some.

My experiences over the years have also helped me to listen to my instincts. There have been times I've been asked to deviate from my usual delivery or do something which I've felt deep in my gut isn't right and sure enough, each time, I realised after that I should have listened to that feeling. I was once asked to deliver a teambuilding session to a large corporate group outside and despite my nagging doubts, I thought 'the customer is always right'. I was right. The participants couldn't hear each other, the session fell flat and we didn't get the intended impact. When I trust my intuition, I know I am on the right track, everything has felt easy and amazing things have happened.

Trust your intuition

Learn to tap back into and trust your instincts. Not the negative inner critic we all get from time to time, but your true intuition

I happily grew Shared Harmonies extensively over the first few years, building a strong corporate client base that includes some of the UK's leading companies and expanding the number of community singing for wellbeing groups, working with people living with Parkinson's, dementia, cancer, poor mental health and respiratory conditions. I appointed freelance staff to help with promotion and delivery of services as demand grew. I was so excited about the future and then... Covid

I remember the day I made the decision to stop my community singing groups and received call after call of cancellations for our corporate work. With the official announcement of the first lock down, I watched everything I had built up and poured my heart into disappear, with no idea when or how it would start again or if we would survive the interruption.

Then I remembered our values. I thought about our participants. I thought about the things people were facing as a result of the pandemic and made a decision – we must help. I set my intentions. One way or another we would continue to deliver services that would keep people connected and uplifted, even if I didn't know how. We couldn't meet in person and I am a complete technophobe but I turned to my team, my tribes, I talked to my participants, and then I took action.

Within 3 weeks we were back up and running. We delivered services through Facebook, Zoom, DVD, phone and reached out to residential care homes and other services supporting those most isolated working through support staff. We co-created new songs, connecting people across the country. We gained new grant funding, won numerous awards and came runner up in the Song for Yorkshire competition. Resilience has been a big part of my entrepreneurial journey. There will always be challenges, it's how I respond to them that makes a difference.

I have noticed the importance of being clear on what I want to achieve. The clearer I have been with my vision, the easier and quicker I have achieved and even surpassed my goals. This was definitely the case during the pandemic. Now we are moving into a new relationship with the pandemic, I am going through a visioning process again, setting my intentions for the next 5 years of Shared Harmonies CIC. It is such an exciting and inspirational process.

Dream big

Aspire to great things, set your intentions, believe it is possible, visualise it and take aligned action.

So where next for us? I see great things ahead for Shared Harmonies CIC. We have come out of the pandemic thriving; our team is growing and is stronger than ever. We have expanded our community services, working in new geographic areas and adding support for people with Long Covid to our existing offer. We are developing projects to support refugees and asylum seekers. We have a range of new workplace wellbeing services to help teams bounce back and avoid burnout. I am excited about our adventures to come.

There is one last lesson I have learnt that I would like to leave you with. I think it's the most important.

Believe in yourself

If you don't, how will anyone else? Be your own biggest champion, believe you can do it and watch incredible achievements come your way

BIO:

Emma Baylin FRSA is a multi-award-winning entrepreneur, writer, speaker and founder of Shared Harmonies CIC. She is a revered trainer and facilitator. She believes passionately in the power of connection and the incredible benefits of singing. Shared Harmonies CIC delivers creative development services for people and communities, enabling participants to make transformational changes. They are proud to have supported leading organisations in the UK and globally.

www.sharedharmonies.co.uk

16

YOU DON'T KNOW WHAT YOU DON'T KNOW

Jenny Lovell

I 've never been particularly ambitious. I mean, I've never strived to be a highflyer, or follow a big salary. I've just wanted to enjoy the job I do and be as good at it as I possibly can. I think I can credit my parents for that. Growing up I was never pressured to try to be top of my class or anything like that. I was simply encouraged to meet my potential. I remember my Dad saying to me, "Jen, it doesn't matter to me if you sweep the streets for a living, just so long as you're the best street sweeper that you can be." That statement set me free in a lot of ways. I did complete my A-levels, and I did go to university, but I never felt under pressure to meet any preconceived expectations. It's certainly how I want my children to feel while growing up.

I have always been a grafter. I can credit that to my family too – and my friends. In fact, everyone I've surrounded myself with over the years has had a really solid work ethic, which has definitely influenced me. I got my first job at 13 (those were the days when you could do that!) and, until I left my last role to set up my business, I'd never been out of employment the whole time. Twenty-seven years of knowing where my next pay cheque was coming from made making the leap to being self-employed a somewhat daunting task, but one I was really excited about and one that just felt right.

My journey into administration began when I was a university student, when my friend's lovely mum gave me the chance of some holiday work in the doctors' surgery where she worked. It was such a brilliant introduction into the world of admin and I met some great characters along the way. The fact that I was trusted with such sensitive information at a relatively young age was something I was really proud of and incredibly grateful for, and I took that responsibility seriously. I soon found my feet there and started to challenge myself to do tasks more efficiently. I felt comfortable in that environment, and it turns out that you can be ambitious within the role you have without having one eye on the next level.

Meanwhile, I was also completing my undergraduate degree in Linguistics at the University of East Anglia. I can't pretend that I was the best student in the world, but I had the best three years of my life, made some amazing lifelong friends, studied a subject that I had passion for, and learnt all about critical thinking and forming supported arguments. I also had the fabulous fortune of meeting my husband, Anthony, in our first year. I had no idea all those years ago that we would still be together now, but he has been my rock and my confidant for the last 23 years and I owe him so much. I certainly couldn't have embarked on the journey of setting up my own business without his unwavering faith and support.

While studying for my degree, my knowledge of and interest

in the nuances of language was deepened by my studies. The fact that language could be manipulated to give not only a specific message, but also a specific feeling or to encourage a certain action was fascinating to me in its subtlety, and something I still feel incredibly passionate about.

My first job after university was as a Customer Care Administrator for a house builder. This was a steep learning curve for so many reasons! I learnt quickly about the build process and more particularly about the customer journey from reservation to final snagging. I didn't own a house at that time, but I empathised with our clients in that they had just made the biggest investment of their life to date and wanted it to be perfect. Although I was occasionally referred to as "Customer don't care" by some particularly disgruntled customers (people tend to lash out at the voice on the phone whether it's their fault or not), I really tried my best to improve processes where possible. This was highlighted when I volunteered – much to everyone's surprise – to take part in a project to improve the customer journey by walking through the process from beginning to end. This included adding/removing steps and reworking all the existing paperwork. I worked with representatives from Build, Sales, Commercial and Finance to gain a full understanding of all the aspects along the way. My participation on this project was met with surprise because I was by far and away the most junior member of the project team, but I wasn't daunted by going head-to-head with directors and managers to get my point across. I just wanted to do the best job that I could and make some changes that I could see would make improvements to the customer experience.

My drive and enthusiasm for embracing change and improvements had me singled out as having a "can do" attitude, and every time I got involved in a new project – often projects I had little prior knowledge of – I was reminded that you don't know what you don't know, and that every day is a school day.

That's a lesson that has never been more pertinent than when you start running your own business. I've learnt so much – and I can't see that changing any time soon!

After carrying out the role of Senior Customer Care Administrator on a caretaker basis for some time, they decided to offer me the role permanently. I politely declined, however, as my husband (then still boyfriend) and I had decided to put an end to our long-distance relationship and move in together. With me still living with my parents in Chester, and he with his family in Southampton, we decided to meet in the middle and move somewhere around Bristol. My honesty about my domestic plans at work were rewarded, and they created a new role for me in our South-west office in Aust as the PA to the Regional Managing Director. I was so flattered that this role had been created for me and I couldn't wait to get stuck in.

I loved my time in the South-west region. The office soon relocated to St Mellons, just outside Cardiff, and we had such a fantastic team there. I carried on my role of change advocate within the region and got involved in the implementation of new software systems and procedures, and generally got involved in as much as I could. I worked closely with the Senior Management Team on using customer feedback to make improvements where possible. I felt very privileged to be a trusted member of this team and loved every minute. Yet again, however, our domestic plans meant that we would soon be making another move. My parents had recently moved to the South Coast, so our Bristol location was no longer halfway between our family bases.

We had also got engaged, so with our impending wedding we decided that we wanted to relocate to be closer to our family and settle in our forever location. So, with regret, I left behind the fantastic team in Cardiff for a role in a large manufacturing organisation in our new home of Hampshire. Culturally it was a big shock, as I'd gone from a relatively small organisation to a relatively large one, but it was a great company. I soon found that there were opportunities everywhere to get involved in new projects and learn about new aspects of the business. It gave me the opportunity to use my degree knowledge and focus my attention on the internal communications.

I was fortunate enough to have supportive Managing Directors who identified that I had more to offer than my role allowed and gave me the platforms to learn and grow. Internal communications were a challenge as we were spread out across several different buildings over different geographic locations, but I enjoyed the challenge and made some real improvements throughout my tenure. During the last few years, however, my personal priorities were completely reorganised. I was blessed with two children (at the time of writing my kids are aged five and three) and we also went through a global pandemic which I think caused us all to realign our personal/professional priorities. If I'm being completely honest with myself, I found that once my daughter started school the juggle of home and work life was becoming more and more challenging. I didn't like the feeling that I had to apologise for each part of my life to the other, and I decided that something needed to change. I had also fallen out of love with my old role, so the time was right for a change.

I honestly believe that without the fantastic network around me the decision to start my business would have been a lot harder. From the initial idea (full credit to my friend Louise for that – I didn't even know what a Virtual Assistant was when she suggested it!), to the advice, support and knowhow from other friends and family along the way, I have had fantastic support. I was lucky enough to hit on a fantastic VA Mentor and network early on (Amanda at VACT), and I have joined a couple of fantastic networking groups which I have found to be very nurturing and supportive too.

It's probably not typical for business owners to admit that

they never dreamed of running their own business – but in all honesty I really didn't think I ever would. I had enjoyed being part of teams and always completely "bought into" the companies that I worked for along the years, so the thought of flying solo had never occurred to me! The reality is that I still get to "buy into" the companies I work for – but it's several different companies at the same time. As I previously said, I wouldn't describe myself as being particularly ambitious, but I am addicted to success, both my own and of those that I support. I realised this would make me perfectly placed to be a cheerleader for my clients and try to help them with the parts of their business that they know are important, but simply don't have the bandwidth to tackle.

I am excited about what the future has to offer. My business has grown quicker than I imagined it would, and my five-year goals now seem more of a reality. I love the variety that my business offers, and I love finding my ideal clients and working out how I can best support them. I have learnt so much since I started, and it makes me realise how siloed I had become working in the same organisation for so long.

I would say that the most important things when starting your own business are having a solid support network, an idea that you have faith in, and an ability to embrace change. It is daunting taking the plunge, but nothing in life that's worth having is easy. It's absolutely true that you don't know what you don't know, but then if you don't give it a try, you never will.

BIO:

Jenny Lovell is a Virtual Assistant and founder of Northern Star VA Ltd. With over 17 years combined experience as a Personal Assistant and Internal Communications Specialist, she is passionate about providing creative and professional support to small businesses to help enable entrepreneurs get back to their passion and business goals. She was born and raised in the North-west of England (Lancashire, Cumbria and Cheshire), but has now settled on the South Coast in Hampshire where she lives with her husband and two young children.

www.northernstarva.co.uk

17

ISN'T IT FUNNY HOW IT ALL COMES TOGETHER?

Romel Peters

It's funny, from a young age I somehow knew being my own boss was inevitable. I always knew I was meant to forge my own path. I had no clue what that path would look like or where it would lead me but something deep inside of my being just knew I was born for something bigger; I was here to make a real impact; I existed because I needed to create something that would change the world in a positive way.

So Romel, how did you begin that journey?

Thanks for asking, but I have a question for you first.

Have you ever reached a point in life where you were just so darn tired? Like, really tired of it all?

Well, that is in fact how my journey of chasing my dream to become a woman in business began.

I really wish I could tell you it began because I found myself having a sudden innovative lightbulb moment whilst drinking a latte in Starbucks. But for me, the drive came when I found myself in tears, crawling across my bedroom floor at 3am in the morning trying to reach my crying son in the other room.

Why was I crawling you ask?

Because I was so FRIGGING TIRED (not the type of tired that required an early night in bed, I was beyond EXHAUST-ED), so much so that I had no energy left in the tank to even walk.

(Don't worry, this story isn't all doom and gloom, *spoiler alert* it has a pretty awesome ending).

As I sat on the carpeted floor of my children's bedroom, cradling my son with a stream of tears running down my face, it was in that very moment I realised I was done! I was so done with:

- Feeling joyless
- Putting my dreams and desires on the back burner because I was too busy supporting others to reach theirs.
- Serving without recognition or acknowledgement.
- Taking on everyone else's crap, putting their wants and needs before my own. Now don't get me wrong, I love my nearest and dearest, but sometimes I just wanted to scream at them. "I have my own problems too. You are big enough to figure this one out on your own, so go put on your big girl/boy pants and handle your shit".
- Having my career progression in the hands of managers who would purposely hold me back in a role I was clearly overqualified for, yet happily pile on extra tasks, those in higher paid positions should've been dealing with.
- Continuing to invest in an unsupportive, toxic, loveless relationship.

You get it, I was done with being tired.

And not only that, but it also broke my heart that my children had not met their 'real' mother. They had never seen the fierce, fun, confident, creative, ambitious, determined woman who once followed her dreams and lived in her purpose. I am quite grateful they were too young to realise at the time that instead, they had been stuck with a miserable, extremely low vibe version of her.

So, what next?

You can guess what I had to do next right?

Honey, I needed to somehow get my groove back. But where to start?

Well...the very next morning I called a moving company.

I told them, "I need to move as soon as possible, what is your earliest availability?"

The man on the phone replied "we can be there by 10am tomorrow "

I was not expecting that response to say the least. And that only gave me just under 24hrs to box up a 2-bedroom house. Oh! and FYI, tomorrow was Christmas eve.

You know what, fuck it! At this point, I have nothing left to lose.

"Ok let's do it, thank you", I replied.

Positivity, positivity, positivity

"Come on Romel, you've got this" I kept saying to myself repeatedly, as I packed up all our belongings, with my 2 children under 2yrs old swinging from my ankles, throwing things out of bags as I had just finished packing them. I must admit though, as stressful as it was having to repack everything, their little faces helped to calm my anxiety and made the process a little easier to manage. I could already see a better life waiting for us on the horizon.

. . .

Fast forward a week or 2

As we settled into the new house, the energy around us completely changed, it was fascinating. The days seemed brighter, my mind was clearer, that feeling of exhaustion was beginning to lift. We were happier.

Wow! Is that what being in a toxic, unhealthy environment was doing to us?

The change in energy felt so liberating, I continued removing myself from anything and anyone that did not contribute to our happiness. I separated myself from everything that no longer aligned with my true values.

I just wanted to feel like me again

After a few months I decided to invest my time in finding inner peace, healing, and learning to master my intuition.

Every single day after putting my children to bed, I would grab a cushion, sit on my living room floor, grab my phone, open the calm app, and do a 10-minute guided meditation.

At first it felt impossible to do, because there was so much noise swirling around in my head, but after remaining consistent, within a couple of weeks I learnt how to quieten the noise and just like that, something truly amazing happened, I began to hear something else...

"I am so proud of you Romel"

"Despite your circumstances, look at everything you have achieved"

"You deserve nothing less than your dreams"

Wait!

What is that?

Who is that?

OMG IT'S HER!

The fierce, ambitious, motivated woman I thought had disappeared almost a decade ago.

She never left, she was with me all along, being drowned out by all the chaos.

The woman I had always admired and dreamt of; was ME!

How did I not see it before?

I could hear, "Romel you were born to shine, you will do magnificent things."

And like magic, life just started piecing itself back together seamlessly.

Whilst out shopping in Tesco one morning, I found myself on the stationery aisle (I never go there). I felt a strong urge to buy a pack of notepads, a folder, and pens.

I got home, unpacked my shopping, placed my new stationery on the table, switched on my laptop and FLIP ME! Straight away a random email popped with a link to register for a women's business summit.

Hell yeah! I signed up without hesitation.

In preparation for the event, I jotted down some business ideas I was interested in pursuing. But one idea stood out.

A few years prior I found a hobby I loved, it was restoring leather footwear back to its original state but adding a customised twist, so it could be a true original piece which reflected the owner's personality. Yes, this is it, I am going to turn my hobby into my first business.

You are the company you keep

I attended every session that summit had to offer. I met some phenomenal women, some who became my mentors. I met my tribe, a group of women who just understood, supported me just because, and poured such light and love into me I couldn't quite fathom it. It was so overwhelming yet comforting.

Being surrounded by such beautiful, genuine souls changed my whole mindset.

I began to see the world differently, I saw myself differently, I showed up differently, I shone differently.

This was it; my dreams and desires were coming to fruition.

I wasn't just dreaming anymore; I was taking action to make it happen. Doors just kept unlocking and my purpose began unfolding.

A new chapter is being written and guess who's holding the pen!?

You got it, Me! And only me!

So where has this chapter taken me so far?

Well, I can tell you for free that in the short space of a year, I am doing so much more than I EVER imagined and this is just the beginning.

8 months after that business summit I found myself organising a launch party to celebrate the grand opening of my Leather Repair and Customising Shop, Eek!

I now have a 2nd business providing coaching services, guiding individuals through their own personal transformation journey. I have created a podcast called 'Familyhood' which is all about breaking down generational cycles within families.

I have spoken at a Virtual Global Summit and finally, I just contributed a chapter to a book, THIS BOOK!

I have only scratched the surface of opportunities, there is much more to come.

The future possibilities are endless, and I cannot wait to discover what the rest of this chapter has in store.

BIO:

Romel is a Mumpreneur, Intuitive Transformational Coach, Mentor, Personal Cheerleader, Aspiring Inspirational Speaker and Podcaster.

To help others avoid reaching a peak level of exhaustion, Romel is dedicated to teaching individuals how to harness their intuition, regain their personal power and control so they can rewrite their reality, and begin to enjoy a full authentic life in alignment with their core values, passion, and purpose.

She's ready to assist anyone who wishes to:

- Top up their self-love tank
- Break free from external controls and expectations
- Heal from past trauma that has contributed to reducing their sense of worthiness
- Reclaim their personal power
- Discover their authentic self

www.romelpeters.com

18

THRIVING BRAND, THRIVING YOU

Lisa Clunie

F rom an early age I loved to draw and be creative. I was always doodling and cutting up magazines with things I liked, creating mood boards and writing imaginative stories. I think it was a natural path for me to be a creative. So, when I went to art college, I was in my element covered in charcoal and paint and experimenting in all aspects of the artistic world. But as soon as I got introduced to graphic design, I knew this was for me.

After my degree I moved to London to be a junior designer at BP and then moved onto Shell International where I became one of their brand managers. It was a fascinating job, making sure that the messaging, look, and feel were always on brand throughout all sectors of the business. Their brand guidelines were huge. As technology developed and more things were becoming digital, changes had to be made to the guidelines, as computers would influence the colours of the logo.

When I had my first daughter, I was torn between my career and being a mum. I was lucky, Shell offered me 2 days a week in the London office and then I could do some freelance work from home in-between. This worked out perfectly. When my 2nd daughter was born, I decided to take a year out, but I missed the creativity, I loved what I did and still do! So, I went freelance, working in London and Southeast agencies, working more hours as the girls got older. I'm so glad I did, as designing was changing at a fast speed, with the internet developing and the digital world becoming the norm. The world was getting smaller, the deadlines became tighter and what the consumer wanted was also changing, brand was becoming more and more important.

In 2012 I started Thrive Studios, a branding and design agency, but as I grew and found out more about my client's businesses, covering a wide range of sectors, I started to realise that what was really needed was the brand strategy. If you had a good strategy in place, then building content and design aspects became so much easier. As social media started to become more popular, showing your brand in a consistent manner was and is crucial. As my businesses grew and I was getting more and more clients, I expanded, taking on staff and premises. This is when my life totally changed! My husband didn't like me being successful and the mental abuse started, but it was a slow process and a drip feed action, small comments which grew and grew. Nothing I did was good enough, I was not looking after the children properly, the house wasn't clean, I had no idea about running a business. You name it I had it thrown back at me. My confidence started to go, and I moved the office back home, got rid of the staff and backed away from the business for a peaceful life at home. I became very anxious, stopped networking, as I would have panic attacks and ended up not being able to speak properly. Then he got a contract away from home, I started to find me again during the week but go backwards at weekends, when he came home. Then one day something hit me, what the hell was I doing with my life and was I really going to let this man control me. No!!! I filed for divorce and became stronger and found me again. He was a narcissist and very controlling, so me divorcing him, did not go down well and it took me 3 and half years to be finely free and nearly bankrupted me. I did a course on positive psychology to help myself, which was fantastic (which now I help my clients with mindset positivity as part of my course).

My work started to pick up and I was advising in brand strategy and brand management, along with hands-on graphic design, within companies and with individuals. Then lockdown came, everything was different, and I had to adapt my business more online. Like many people, zoom was my lifeline! My main projects that time of year were AGMs, conferences, and exhibitions, that all stopped, deadly silence! So once again in my life I had to think outside the box to find new work and connect with new people. Networking was perfect!

While networking throughout lockdown, I got to meet some amazing people but really noticed that a large proportion of them were in their 40s, 50s and even 60s. They were starting their businesses or were adapting them, and they did not have a clue what branding could do for them or what branding actually was. IT IS NOT your logo or website, it is 'what people say when you are not in the room'. You want people to have an emotional connection with your brand, building that trust and connecting with them. Think of a brand as a person, everyone has their own personality, way of dressing, communicating, their own values, friends, characteristics, and story to tell. It is this that makes up who we are, and it is also these characteristics that make a brand. It's what makes your company different from the competition. For example: If no brand design was applied to bottled water, the consumers would buy just water and any water, it doesn't matter which as they all look the same, it's just clear liquid. But with branding you make your product different, it is the reason a consumer walks into the super-market and purchases one brand over another. The companies build a lifestyle around that water, a brand story and their messaging and tone of voice is consistent. It is therefore not just the physical features that create a brand but also the feelings that consumers develop towards the company or its product. This combination of physical and emotional connections is trig-gered when exposed to the name, logo, visual identity and the message behind the brand.

It doesn't matter how small or large your company is, we all have a brand, good or bad. But you need to build a brand that attracts your ideal audience. In a survey by Zendesk, 87% of consumers said that consistent branding across all online and traditional platforms was important. This means that customers expect that your brand is the same over email, website, customer service, and every touchpoint in your business.

When you are starting a business or already have a business, it can feel like there are a million pieces to pull together: the strategy, the vision, the language, not to mention the visuals. Spending time networking with people, I knew I could work with them to untangle their brand to give them clarity and build a brand that had purpose. So, 'Thriving Brand' was born, to guide and mentor people, and companies, on how to build a brand in all aspects from the foundations and beyond.

Many of my clients feel like their brand doesn't match who they are as a person, let alone attracting their ideal clients! They have a lack of clarity, which is holding them back from taking action and showing up online. Sometimes they are not completely clear on their ideal client and therefore their message isn't clear. Mostly they are feeling overwhelmed and not sure what direction to move forward. They need to have a brand which reflects their expertise, with their true style and voice. And they want to stand out from the noise, get noticed and attract their dream clients. They want a brand that gives them goosebumps, a smile on their face and one they are proud of and points to their future goals.

So how do you do this? Think about why you started your business, what are your goals and what makes you unique from everyone else? What is your brand story, its personality? Who are your target audience, do you have a niche? (Remember not everybody is your ideal audience!) Does your brand need to be understood better, loved more and memorable for all the right reasons? These are the things that bring you more business and make your value shine, allowing you to charge more for what you do.

People do business with people, so how you come across as a personal brand these days is important. It's a common misconception that personal branding is 'something for the younger generation'. In fact, personal branding and the impact you make is relevant to everyone, of any age, gender and occupation. This has become even more so with Covid, people crave the human, personal approach and want to connect and interact. You need to be YOU on social media, authentic and true, not be someone you are not (as you will get found out and lose your audience's trust). Sometimes we forget as we get older, how much expertise we have, how much knowledge we have consumed. I help my clients find their voice, give them clarity, break through those self-doubts and build a clear brand story that is them, that they are proud of, and can show up with confidence. Plus earn that money they deserve.

I've learnt through my business and personal life that you evolve and grow. Your brand will change and adapt as your business develops and so will you. We are resilient, strong and I am extremely lucky to do a job that I love and help others to build a business for themselves, with a little help from me of course! (Smiling emoji)!

. . .

BIO:

Lisa has worked in branding and design for over 25 years, working with international corporates to agencies in London. She set up her own Design agency in 2012 but soon realised that it was brand strategy that was really needed to help businesses to grow and stand out in this crowded and noisy world. Lisa set up 'Thriving Brand' as a brand coach and mentor, working with start-ups to small-medium sized companies, working either 1:1 or in groups, running workshops, online training and speaking at events. With her passion, creativity and enthusiasm she is determined to help you understand your customers, transform their experience and ensure you secure the benefits. Now she wants to help other women, especially in their 40's, 50's and 60's+, find who they are through all aspects of branding whether that is personal brand or for business. To build a strong brand that shows their values, giving them confidence to show up and be themselves and watch them grow and thrive.

www.thrivingbrand.com

19

UNLEASH THE POWER OF YOUR BRILLIANCE

Coylette James

S ome of the stories you are reading in this book are women who are hugely successful and have been in business for years. This is not yet my story. I say not yet because I am starting a new chapter in my life, and I know that the day is coming when I too will be able to say these things about the business successes in my life.

In the meantime, let me introduce myself to you. I am a somewhat late bloomer to this society of successful business-women. This is not for lack of trying earlier on in life to start a business. In fact, I have started a few. I had my own line of greeting cards, did dropship fashions, and sold health products through network marketing, just to name a few of my endeavors. None of these took hold to the place of being self-sustaining and as they say, life happens.

Being the head of household as a single mother for me meant keeping a job and not taking the risk of pursuing dreams if it involved not having a steady income. Then there was the on again off again seesaw of a rocky marriage which meant not being able to depend on my mate to support me whilst I pursued a business. After the marriage stabilized, then my husband's health started to fail and he could no longer work, so again, I found myself not in a position to risk the business gamble.

Now here I am at 65 and at a place of all or nothing in my life. The problem with the other entrepreneurial ventures I did was that they were never my passion. Had they been, then I would have put my all into them and not looked at it as an expendable commodity. I did enjoy creating greeting cards but to say I was passionate about it, would be untrue. When you are not all into what you are doing, then it becomes very easy to walk away from it.

When passion meets purpose, then magic happens. It is like powering up an engine. When that battery cable hits the post, the engine roars. Last year I launched my passion for speaking into the lives of others to encourage them to be the very best they can be. The results have been amazing. Doors have opened that I would have never dreamed of happening so quickly in this phase of my journey.

I want to encourage you to find your passion and through it, part of your purpose will be revealed. I say part of it because your purpose will be tied to specific assignments given you by your creator. There will be many different assignments, each with their own unique set of circumstances, but you will be the answer for each one of them. I don't know your belief system, but mine is that of a woman of Strong Faith in God. I believe that we were created on purpose for purpose, and we need to be walking in that purpose.

The purpose of a thing can only be found in the mind of the creator of it. If you don't know the purpose of something, then you will abuse it or abnormally use it. To misuse ourselves is a far to common thing we do. I did it for many years before I realized that I was not just something to be used for others gratification with no regard for who I was as a person. When you were created, it was not a mistake, and it was not just because your mother and father had physical relations. It was because you were to be an answer for specific problems or situations to come.

When you think about entrepreneurship, businesses are started to solve a problem. If a business is not fulfilling a need, it will soon close its doors. If the business is not of quality and integrity the same fate will befall it. This is why it is important to link your passion with your purpose when establishing your business. Passion will cause you to ensure everything connected to the business is done in excellence. Passion will not allow you to throw in the towel and walk away. Every time you feel discouraged, your passion will ignite the flame within you to keep going.

As I shared above, I am at a stage in life that my why has to align with my how. At 65 to be honest, most people are looking for retirement options. I was looking for longevity and legacy options. If I am to be transparent here, I don't have a pension to fall back on, and the little governmental assistance my country gives to its elderly would not be enough for me to continue the lifestyle to which I am accustomed.

There is no age limit to pursuing your passion. In fact, for some of us it is better later. Our younger selves would not be able to properly handle our newfound prosperity or notoriety. The older we get, the more comfortable we become in being ourselves and being responsible for the abundance we have. We tend to take off the mask we have worn for years while trying to please everyone other than ourselves. When I show up now, I am unapologetically myself. I have done the inner work to find out who I am at my core and no longer allow the pains and disappointments of my past to govern my present or future.

For women, we in so many instances, have had to allow life to get out of our way in order to embrace our dreams. We have been wives, mothers and caregivers, all while secretly hiding our inner ambition to create a different life. Not to say the things we have accomplished in rearing our children and caring for our elderly parents has not been gratifying. It has, but there has always been that dream of something else in the back of our mind and in our heart.

Now is the time for me to step into my purpose and passion in talking with you. I need to speak to that place within you where you have hidden your desire for more because it may signal your life has been unfulfilled. I don't want to sound cliché here, but all that you have accomplished thus far is wonderful, however, "THE BEST IS YET TO COME"!

My gift and purpose is to help you Unleash the BRILLIANCE of who you truly are outside of what you have done up to this point. Yes, there is an entrepreneur within you. No, it is not too late for you to pursue your dream of owning your own business. If Grandma Moses could start to paint at 76, if Toni Morrison could explode on the literary scene with a Nobel Prize for literature at 62 and live to 88 and see her work on the silver screen many times over, if Evelyn Gregory could become a flight attendant at 71 after her husband died, if Jacqueline Murdock at age 82 could see her dream of becoming a Model in Paris, then you can absolutely see your dream come into fruition of being an entrepreneur at your age!

First things first, what are you passionate about? What would you do even if nobody paid you to do it? These are important questions to answer on your journey to answering your call to be a business owner. Why, because there may be times when you will do it for free. Your passion will call upon you to give of yourself. I love teaching, it is my fivefold spiritual gift. I have taught Christians how to incorporate the spiritual things of God with the natural things of business to achieve supernatural success since 2005. I loved doing it, and for the most part I did it for free. My three-hour long Kingdom Empowerment Seminars were not only beneficial to my attendees, but I also now realize they were training for me to be comfortable on bigger stages doing what I do now. Never despise small beginnings.

I was fortunate to grow up in an entrepreneurial home. You could say it's in my blood to own my own business. My mother was a cosmetologist and owned her own salon. I grew up being taught that nothing was impossible for me. I may have to work harder or a bit longer to see my dream fulfilled as a woman of color, but if I applied myself to what I wanted, then I could achieve it. Problem was that my path in life was very different than my mother's who had my father to back her up and already had her own business before they adopted me.

Being a teenage mother at 14, second child at 16 made my path a bit more difficult, however, it did not make it an impossibility. I don't know what your pain point has been in stepping out to accomplish your goals, but I do know you are well able to achieve them. No matter how large the goal is, it starts with the first step of saying I will.

Unleashing the POWER of your BRILLIANCE requires you to come face to face with your unique self and believe in the value and worth you bring to the table. You have to believe in yourself if you want others to believe in you. You are your brand no matter what field you endeavor to go into. You represent your company to your clients, buyers and employees therefore you need to be authentic in who you are.

Next, you have to plan your strategy. I am still working my job in addition to working my business. I make a six-figure salary which I am grateful for, but I treat it as a means to an end. Using my income from my job to finance the upstart of my business is part of my strategy. Make sure you are using wisdom in your business moves. Count up the cost of setting up your business for success. What must you have in place to make your company sustainable for the long term?

There will be investments that have to be made, in you, and in your business. Don't cut corners in the preparation of your success. Remember, you get what you pay for. If you are not willing to invest in yourself along with your business, then you are setting yourself up for failure. A leader is only as valuable as the knowledge they possess. Know your business, but also make sure you know yourself, which includes your strengths and weaknesses. Strengths will tell you what you are able to accomplish yourself, weaknesses will tell you where you need to hire someone to help you.

Arise and shine and allow the GREATNESS within you to ILLUMINATE from you and unleash the POWER of your BRILLIANCE in the business world. Many are waiting for the answer you possess!

BIO:

Recognized as a powerful Speaker, Teacher and Role Model with a gift for connecting with people on all economic, social and age levels, Dr. Coylette James impacts many lives.

The founder of Kingdom Influencer Life, she is currently encouraging Leaders to become agents of Influence creating living legacies. In addition to the living legacy message, is the Unleash the POWER of your BRILLIANCE as you Embrace your UNIQUENESS platform.

As a Minister of the Gospel, she is promoting entrepreneurship through her Kingdom Empowerment Seminars, which encourages Christians to incorporate the Spiritual things of God with the Natural things of business to achieve SUPER-NATURAL success.

Prior to launching her speaking career, Dr. James worked for famed boxing promoter Don King for 28 years. This experience has enhanced her abilities to relate to people on every level and in all walks of life.

You can connect with her across all social media as Coylette James.

www.kingdominfluencer.life

PAINT YOUR OWN RAINBOW

Kellie Williams

I'm delighted to be writing this for you and I hope that my chapter inspires you to take that step, start that business or scale your existing business and 'paint your own rainbow'.

When I was growing up my brother was the academic one and I was the dancer. My brains were in my feet! Or so we thought... I went on to have a very successful recruitment career however, I always knew there was something more out there for me.

My story starts in 2019. I was a Branch Manager for a Healthcare Recruitment company achieving great things but not feeling valued. My husband Simon and I have 2 children - Emily and Thomas. Our life was nice, but we were time poor and had to say no to the children a lot when it came to sports, clubs and play dates which are all so important at their age and you don't get this time back. I must admit we were coping but the cracks were starting to show.

Then came my dad's dementia diagnosis. He had been showing symptoms for a while and mum and I had suspected it but this kind of diagnosis not only majorly impacts the individual but hits family members like a tonne of bricks, along with the worry that Frontal Temporal Lobe Dementia can be hereditary.

Dad is an entrepreneur and successful businessman. A talented builder who was always able to design, build and fix things with a great interest in computers. His condition started to deteriorate quickly.

So, picture this... I was extremely busy running an office, managing 3 members of office staff and 100 care staff, I'd grown the revenue from £5k per week to £20k per week and doubled the profit margins. I had built a team and a business, I was working silly hours and looking after a busy on-call phone. But it wasn't mine!

By this point towards the end of 2019, I was realistic about the situation:

- My children needed me therefore I needed flexibility
- My dad's dementia was only going to get worse – he needed me, and my mum needed support
- The business I had built was not mine

I'm welling up writing this as I'm telling my story. Something had to give!

I was headhunted along with my team which was all very exciting at the time but I very quickly realised I'd made the wrong decision. I quickly went on to make another poor decision by accepting another role only a few months later. This was sticking on a plaster and on day three I drove to the office and posted my keys through the letterbox. Dramatic with a capital D and with a side of jazz hands thrown in!

. . .

The Hats!

My mind started racing. I had always wanted to run my own business and now was the time. I thought about all my skills, experience, industries I had worked in and what I could offer to potential clients. I started to consider who I wanted to help. People like me, busy parents who were working, people who were time poor and needed support. I thought about business owners wearing all the hats and falling down the rabbit hole. The 80's TV show 'The A Team' was also playing over and over in my head.

Twenty-four hours later the idea for At the Drop of a Hat was born and within one month I had launched my Virtual Assistant business.

Then came the scaling

Everything went well and I started gaining clients straight away but there was something missing. I realised that I was missing mentoring and managing a team. It can be lonely when you start a business.

In March 2020 I started my matching service (not agency!). My 'zone of genius' is business development and although VA's are very talented at what they do many of them struggle to grow their businesses. I saw a gap in the market and went for it.

By June 2020 things were really taking off and I hired my first VA to work on my business. This simple act of outsourcing proved to be successful, and my revenue and profits increased by 300%!

I was coming into my own and starting to gain confidence. The business was now gaining momentum, so I ran with it and launched a course and membership in February 2021. This is when I really started enjoying each part of my business. The course and membership were linking to the matching service, and this was evolving into a consultancy.

The most successful entrepreneurs all promote having several income streams which is why I have added different services, passive and semi-passive income and affiliate programs to my portfolio.

Writing the course whilst delivering it in March 2021 was challenging but very enjoyable. The mentor in me really thrived. Being able to support others on their business journey is so rewarding. Many people who join the course are busy parents craving a more flexible life.

Once the course was written I took the sensible decision to make it evergreen. I recorded the modules and created an online portal. This now forms part of the strategy work I do with clients in my consultancy to help them build semi-passive and passive income products.

Fast forward to July 2021 and I had achieved it! I was now able to refer to At the Drop of a Hat as a six-figure business!

It may sound crazy, but I celebrated going VAT registered and setting up my limited company. Now don't get me wrong this journey was not all champagne and roses - none of this landed in my lap. I have worked hard, I have made lots of mistakes, I have had bad luck but most of all I became confident and resilient.

I am a solutions provider; I love puzzles and a challenge in business. My Dad has always said "Experience is what you get when you don't get what you want!". Use the feeling and channel it.

Lifestyle

Here we are in 2022 and I'm writing this on my 45th birthday. I'm so proud to tell you that I have achieved happiness and contentment.

The lifestyle I have now was exactly what I had wanted

when I put those keys through the letterbox of the office in 2020.

I make my own decisions about my diary. I am incredibly lucky to work with the most amazing team. I delegate to my amazing OBM/work wife Emily and my Social Media Manager and long-standing friend Emma.

These incredible humans make it possible for me to dedicate my time to my children. I'm now able to take Thomas to football training 4 times a week and football matches at the weekend which means everything to me.

My Dad's condition is progressing which we always expected. This is so tough to watch but now I'm able to spare more time to take my dad out and give my mum some much needed downtime making memories whilst we can. My brother and his wife have also moved back to Chester. This has taken the weight off my shoulders as they are here and dedicated to supporting the family.

I have some amazing clients. My workdays are varied, not one day is the same and every day I learn something new. I am developing as a business owner and mentor. I will never know everything but what I learn along the way I can pass on to clients and VA's.

My mission is to help inspire as many people as possible. There is a different way. You can start a new venture and make it a success. You can create the life you dream of and fit your work around your life rather than the other way around.

So, if you are reading this and what I am saying resonates with you, you dream of a different lifestyle, you know you have more to give and you don't want to wait any longer then this is your time to 'paint your own rainbow'.

If you are thinking of becoming a VA grab a notebook and pen and write down:

What your current lifestyle looks like

Your dream lifestyle

Your goals

All the jobs you have had

Tasks you can do

Systems you have experience using

Industries you have worked in

What you could offer to potential clients and how you could help them

If you are a busy business owner thinking of hiring a VA grab a notebook and pen and write down:

All the tasks in your business

Highlight all the tasks that only you can do

The rest you will be able to delegate to the perfect VA

Are you thinking of adding passive or semi-passive income streams to your business?

Ideas for courses

Ideas for memberships

Ideas for subscription boxes

This is me

Successful six-figure business owner and VA Mentor

I was a professional dancer and had the best time travelling the world

I'm married to Simon, and we have two amazing children Emily and Thomas

My Dad has Dementia

We have a cat called Buttercup

I love Marmite!

Mine's a prosecco

I'm pretty sure I was a Mermaid in a previous life as I love the sea and my favourite food is seafood and shellfish!

I am fiercely loyal and will run to the end of the earth for my friends

Don't interrupt me when Strictly is on!

My Mum is a dancer and so was my grandma

I am a recovering control freak and getting to grips with this has helped me scale my business.

BIO:

Kellie is a qualified dance teacher and danced her way around the world before meeting her husband and settling down in North Wales with their two children Emily and Thomas.

Kellie had a successful 15-year recruitment career. She specialised in developing business and making branches profitable.

She launched At the Drop of a Hat Ltd in 2019 providing support to busy business owners with her team of Virtual Assistants, Online Business Managers, Designers and Copywriters .

Now running a six-figure business Kellie supports clients and mentors VA's so they can achieve their goals.

www.atthedropofahat.co.uk

21

COLLECTING SEASHELLS

Tilly Wilson

This all started with a lantern.

I've always had a love of home interiors. When we moved to our new house I had a blank canvas to be as creative as I wanted. I loved every second of planning and bringing together all the pieces for our new home.

In the middle of 2020 I was prepping the garden and I wanted some lanterns to dot around to create a warm atmosphere in the evenings. I'm a great lover of finding pieces you can't necessarily get on the high street and I'd fallen in love with some lanterns I'd seen on Instagram. Unfortunately, they were out of stock everywhere, but after searching the internet, I eventually found some and promptly ordered several to add that finishing touch. They arrived and I was delighted with them and the compliments I got as a result.

During those summer evenings, the more I looked at the

lanterns, the more I thought about how I would love to run an online store like the one I'd purchased them from.

I mentioned it to my husband Barry...

"Do it then?" he said.

"I couldn't run my own business, don't be daft."

"Of course you could, I'll help you" he replied.

And that was the point which kicked it all off.

A couple of months later, we sat at home with my stepson Jack and daughter Lillia, who was 8 at the time, talking about how I could begin the process of setting up the business. Jack had recently graduated with a business degree and had lots of enthusiasm and Lillia was immediately full of ideas.

First things first - a name. We thrashed a few weird and wonderful ideas about, but nothing hit the spot. Then Lillia said, "Mummy, you should call it Collecting Seashells."

It was perfect and had the meaning I was searching for. Our homes are a reflection of us, telling our story. For us, the seashells that Lillia and I collect together from our holidays and display around our home do just that. They are beautiful reminders of the memories we've shared together. And that's what I wanted the business to be all about.

We knocked up a crude version of our logo, registered the company, bought the domain and set up the social media in that one evening, it really was that quick.

And Collecting Seashells was born.

What a whirlwind it has been since then!

I'll be honest, I didn't expect it to be as hard as it was. We've always had our own businesses but it's my husband who has always been at the helm, with me supporting. I suppose taking care of the family has always been my number one role. I looked after all the other business bits, but I'd never had the spotlight shone directly on me.

I think I started this with naivety, that this would be a simple process. I'd set up a website and Instagram page, take some nice pictures and bang, orders would come flooding in. The reality was far from that.

In the early days, I really did feel like an imposter - I couldn't do this and who was I trying to kid. The list of things to do was ever growing and my ability to tick things off was getting harder and harder. I was overwhelmed and drowning. Pouring hours and hours in, and getting little done, all at the expense of family time. I had serious mum guilt and there were times when I regretted ever starting this venture.

However, my husband, not a fan of 'feeling sorry for yourself', but big fan of the 'tough love', gave me some clear insights into my shortcomings and didn't sugar coat it. It wasn't easy to hear, and as much as I wanted to resent him for it, I knew it was coming from a place of love, protection and, of course, experience. He could see clearly from the outside where I was going wrong.

I was five months down the line and hadn't achieved anything. I had no website, no stock, no processes, no idea whether I was coming or going and was expecting to launch in a month's time. It was madness. But that reality check was exactly what I needed, I got myself organised and got to work!

My stepdaughter Toria and husband Shaun were the ground workers on this for me. It was great me wanting a pretty e-commerce site, but they had to make it a reality. They built the entire site from scratch, spent endless hours tweaking and testing. Without them, we would never have got it off the ground and I'm so grateful to have had them in my corner.

I then had to focus on getting stock and suppliers - what a strange experience! Some wholesalers are a bit protective and can be cagey about letting you in at first. At some points it was like trying to join a secret society! I thought I would just be able to call up and ask for an account, what I hadn't expected was that I would have to sell myself to be allowed to stock their products! I was an e-commerce business with no website, no stock, no suppliers, no trade references so, boy, did I have to sell it! I managed to get the majority of wholesalers on board so I could finally start sourcing gorgeous stock to sell.

I loved this part (who wouldn't!), and it was a real joy to finally press the button on this. That's when it felt most real, it really was happening.

And then… the boxes started arriving and kept arriving. My house, garage and loft turned into a storage unit pretty much overnight! Everywhere you turned there was stock, I was constantly checking in or sending back returns, you couldn't move for boxes. I was definitely not popular, everyone in my house had had enough of Tilly, her boxes and Collecting Seashells!

One of the days I laugh about the most was the day the bubble wrap arrived. Endless rolls of it turned up at my front door. They were everywhere, filling the house from front to back. It was like a forest of giant six-foot bubble wrap trees and all I could think about was that Barry was going to flip out if he got home and saw it! So, we got them out of the house as quickly as we could and into the garage, like nothing ever happened!

Up until launch it was all hands on deck. Everyone was doing something. Ordering boxes, uploading stock, dealing with SEO, writing product descriptions, T&Cs with the lawyer and adding the finishing touches to website. Then at 8pm on 26th April, the site went live. We had done it. We popped some champagne and I cried. We even got some orders that night. It did feel amazing.

But that was just the start. I thought that the hardest part would be setting it all up, however I was about to undergo a much steeper learning curve than I had ever imagined.

Lots of very late nights packaging up deliveries, utter desperation at trying to figure out what Google wants, zero time for anything and lots of tears and exhaustion followed.

Again, Barry gave me some more valuable guidance and it was clear I couldn't do this all on my own.

I needed to stop trying to do everything and get help to run this business. I was lucky enough to have Katie come on board as GM. She has been an incredible source of help and support, giving me the space to recover my work/life balance. Being a mum and looking after my family will always be my number one job and having control over this again was a gift.

Having said that, it still can be all-consuming. There's plenty of late nights and worry, but I suppose that's what comes from growing a business. I was definitely naïve to think it would be an easy ride to success, but I feel now I'm able to enjoy what I'm doing whilst being so passionate about it. The hard work is validated every time someone buys our products. It's then that I really know I'm getting it right.

So here I am now, fast approaching the end of my first year of trading and I'm still standing.

Starting your own business is an incredibly hard thing to do, but not impossible.

It doesn't happen overnight, it never does. All successful businesses out there are a result of hard work and determination. So, if you think it's as easy as starting an Instagram page and then you're a big hit, think again. And once you accept that, things do get easier.

We built a brand from the ground up in six months (in what I now understand is a very short space of time to do something like this) and, my goodness, the things we got wrong.

But my goodness, the things we got right!

It's hard work, you have to graft. And although my work/life lines get blurred on many occasions, I want my Lillia to have that work ethic I do. I want her to know that there is a world of opportunity out there, but it doesn't get handed to you, you have to work hard, and it comes with sacrifice.

So, what have I learned in my first year?

Well, I've learned that I can't do everything myself and how to release things to others to do. Do the things you're good at and stop trying to be a control freak.

I've learned to listen to my husband and not the voice inside my head saying you're not good enough to do this.

I've learned to not compromise standards. Don't accept things that aren't good enough or do things on the cheap, it's always more costly in the long run.

I've learned that you have to plan and be organised and with Barry's revelation of my untidy mind ringing in my ears… make lists and get yourself organised. It really is the key.

I've learned to be grateful for family time more than ever and not to take that precious time for granted. Little ones are little for such a short time, drink up every ounce of it that you can. And on the days when you're all tapped out, remember what is really important to you and what you're doing this for.

I've learned that you have to be the face of your business and you must be genuine. As much as people are buying your products, they have to buy into you and your story. Don't fake it, they'll see right through you.

Most of all, I've learned that you have to take it easy on yourself. You can't beat yourself up every time you hit a wall or something goes wrong. There's no one out there who will be harder on you than you. So, remember to be kind, honest with yourself and realistic about your goals. There will always be obstacles and things that knock you, but great things never come from comfort zones, so dust yourself off, put your big girl pants on and go again.

I now stock and sell those lanterns on my own website.

BIO:

Online home décor boutique Collecting Seashells is a haven full of hand-selected treasures, each picked with the vision of creating lasting memories throughout the home.

Founder Tilly Wilson had a dream to combine her passion for home accessories with a keen eye for interiors. The result was Collecting Seashells, which launched in April 2021. By bringing together beautiful pieces and the latest trends, buyers can expect to find carefully selected products which create unique spaces and help reflect their personality throughout the home. It's the little touches that create authentic spaces which genuinely mirror people who live there and tell their story.

www.collectingseashells.com

22

CHASE THE MOON AND THE STARS

Stevie McCormick

Y ou are made for more and my soul's mission is to show you how to start living your wild, free, and limitless life.

Let me tell you my story. Not so long ago I had forgotten my soul's mission. I had quickly made my way up the corporate ladder in a shiny Business and Development Senior Management Role. By the age of 22 I had landed my first management position and by 25 I was sat on a senior management team.

But the office, fancy job, and team, was accompanied with fancy holidays, nice car, house, and things. Yet there I was still feeling dissatisfied. My heart ached. I thought 'there has got to be more than this'.

In June 2019 whilst sorting and prepping one of the offices for a move, I picked up a box and there was a *swoosh*. A table landed on my foot. I yelped and hobbled across the offices to my chair, screaming 'I'm fine I just need a minute' to everyone who was asking me if I was okay with a mix of concern and confusion.

As people peered through the office door at me saying, 'we think you need to go to hospital' which I bravely refused. The tough cookie; that's me. I was soon whisked off in a colleague's car when it finally dawned on me that I had broken my big toe!

The next day I was sat at home with my feet up, a broken toe (and soul) thinking 'oh no what next?'.

This really was a sign from the universe to stop! At this point my Saturn return was kicking in. Saturn is the planet of structure and authority you have two during your lifetime. One at 30 and one at around the age of 60. The planets align to restructure areas of your life to bring you back into true alignment with your values and the desires you wish to create on this earth. During these time frames you can leave relationships, create new careers, and completely change the direction of your life and values.

Leading up to this point I had become a kind of closet spiritual witch. I am not going to lie. I always had a crystal around my neck or on my desk at work. However, I wasn't out there with it. I was successful and driven in my career, but I couldn't shake the feeling that I should be on a different path. I wanted to pour my heart into something I loved. I could never quite figure it out.

Let's just say I have always been determined to rewrite the judgement others had of me. I had managers who told me I was "too much". Despite these comments, a year later I was asked to lead an inspiring woman's talk at the Springboard Development Programme within that organisation.

Before gaining my senior role, I had one recruiting manager at the same organisation say you are under-skilled and don't have enough experience, try aiming a little lower. In true Stevie style I was determined to show I could do anything I put my mind to. Ten applications later I landed a job 5X higher than the salaried job that I was told I wasn't good enough for in the same organisation.

When I left home at 16 they said she will end up pregnant and need support. She will never make it. I followed my soul and left a toxic environment and took care of me first. This is where a lot of my approval issues were stemming from; an unsupportive family background.

I had been reconnecting with my inner child through therapy, in all honesty on the quest of gaining family approval, to do things right and follow the path of life. You know, the one where you secure the 9-5 job, mortgage, living quietly inside the edges. It dawned on me the love and acceptance from them wasn't forthcoming and I needed to love myself first. I had lost sight of what **Stevie** wanted to do. I felt more lost than ever.

During these therapy sessions, I remembered I wasn't just placed on this earth to work hard and gain approval. I began on a journey to find myself again and it didn't take long for crystal collecting, spell making and dreamy inner Stevie to take centre stage.

Within me lived this passionate star and moon gazer, world healer, empath and a wild soul who was destined to run free.

I couldn't bear to be under the constraints of rigid 9 to 5 work any longer. I am someone who knows that I am here to create and lead a world where everyone can shine within their own unique gifts to live wildly and abundantly on their own terms with no rule book.

There I was: corporate officer by day and witch by night holding moon ceremonies, manifesting my dream life and charging my crystals. There was always an ache in my heart and the 'big toe drama' shifted a lot. After that incident I was only at work a few days a week, breaking the 9-5 routine.

As I began to increase my hours of returning to work, panic attacks began to creep in and my feelings of dissatisfaction came to a head. One day as I quietly took myself off to the bathroom for a quick secret weep one of the senior management team caught me and led me to her office.

I poured my heart out, 'I can't do this anymore, I feel like I am dying.' I've found a job but it's so much less money than I am on but it's a start to try and figure out what I really want to do. I openly debated my actions and thoughts in the room with her.

She quickly loaded the job up on her PC and said 'You've got to do it Stevie. This is your stepping stone.'

With that I passionately completed the application form with a twinkle in my soul. I have so got this, I said to myself. 2 weeks later I had the interview and was immediately phoned by them to say they were blown away by my interview and how soon could I join them.

I skipped my way to my car to drive home that night and gathered my thoughts to tell my employer, because despite the feelings of dissatisfaction, I had a deep love and bond with my team and what I had created through my corporate role. It was truly a rebirth, a letting go of the old and so much of me was tied up in this job. I was ready for a fresh start.

My team were all thrilled for me and I had the most wonderful send off. With that I began as a health and wellbeing trainer, taking a big pay cut. However, I managed to negotiate the pay. I rewrote my next chapter with a heart on a mission of figuring this spiritual awakening out.

Around the time I was in therapy I had set up an Instagram account as I had a vision of healing people. My intention was to begin to build this to run alongside my other job as I now had more headspace to figure it out. I started my new job in January 2020. 6 weeks after training, guess what came... the pandemic!

Just like that I was gifted time beyond my wildest imagination. I sometimes joke that I manifested the pandemic. In all my future scripting (this is a great practice where you write in future tense what you wish to happen). By this point I had written about having copious amounts of time at home to create my dream life and there I was with all this time and space to create.

I began to network, create content, workshops, connections, exchange work for others to gain testimonials for my work. Clients and work began to get busier and at last I had found my niche.

I studied and read about marketing and entrepreneurship. Running it on my own felt like a whole new world. Both terrifying and exciting at the same time.

I would come off from zoom calls with clients with a spring in my step. As a result of my work, people were handing in their notices, earning more money, creating more confidence in their business, finding their purpose, sorting out problems in their relationships, creating their own businesses, healing from past trauma. The outcomes were endless. My phone would ping with their updates of how our work together had transformed their lives. Because I was connecting them to their why, their belief system and giving them space to believe everything they dreamt of was possible.

They would step away confident and clear. My heart felt alight and inspired all day!

By April 2021 I reduced my working hours. I had to take a leap of faith but always wondered when I would hand in my notice in my day job.

In July 2021 we lost our house bunny Thumper, he was a big part of my journey and therapy. As he, alongside my husband Billy, my in-laws Diane and Caz and Dotty their dog made me feel like I had my own little family where I was loved, supported, and nourished. He taught me how to put myself first. When I had down moments he would sit at my feet. He kept me going on days where I thought I couldn't carry on.

With his departure I felt a real sense of how quickly 8 years of his life had gone by. I logged onto a zoom meeting and one of my team members announced they had handed in their notice and were due to leave in 6 weeks' time. My heart sank and as soon as the meeting finished, I ran to the toilet and was sick.

Three weeks earlier under the full moon I had prewritten my notice letter. I remember that it was before the end of July I had noted on the letter I would hand it in. I recall the dread as the days approached and July ticked by. I thought, it won't happen this month, but time was running out.

Little did I realise as I opened the letter it was dated the 27th of July and that was the day I handed it in!

It was a good sign; I apprehensively started an email to my manager and before I knew it, I pressed send (if you scroll on my Instagram @starsbystevie, you will find the video).

With that, I was free.

BIO:

Stevie is now the proud Director of Stars by Stevie full time. She is a highly sought-after motivational speaker, mentor, and coach to aspiring ambitious women who are ready to speak from their truest voice and connect deeply to their intuition to lead a life and business on their terms, rule book free.

As a qualified Learning and Development Professional and Astrologer Stevie combines her unique knowledge of psychology, energy healing work and mindset to create group and 1-2-1 programmes. She continues to support and empower others to gain a deeper self-awareness of their true authentic self, to create a successful life and business they deserve. At the time Stevie wrote this chapter she has supported and inspired over 250 women and her business is growing day by day. She has led them to claim their dreams and ambitions to create a life and business they love on their terms.

She continues to pour her heart and soul into her work with a head full of dreams still at her feet. You'll find Stevie on a Dorset beach running along the sand, finding shells and swimming in the sea with her cockapoo Ted and husband Billy. She's the type of girl the stars wish for and the moon chases and so are you. Remember, everything is possible when you believe in yourself!

www.starsbystevie.com

23

DISCOVERING JOY IN THE JOURNEY

Jessica Jarels

D o you believe that you are the leading role of your story? That you have power and purpose, in this present moment? Do you believe, with your whole being, that you were made to shine?

When the idea of writing a book popped into my head a few weeks ago, it scared me. It would require me to step out and shine, and that was nerve-wracking. Two weeks later, I'm participating in the Women Thrive Summit and find myself on a Trudy Simmons' seminar. An opportunity to write my story presents itself. I couldn't stop thinking about it, so I reached out to her and said yes, I want to write something.

I reviewed the paperwork and noticed that it talks about stories of women and their business journey. I immediately backpedal, telling her that I should wait because I don't have a "business" and that my story is more about my journey to discovering my passion. I even tell her "maybe I should wait until it is all revealed and I have a website up and running." To which she so graciously responds "JESSICA…it is totally up to you – BUT – you said this was something you wanted to do… DO IT. Your story needs to be heard…"

This is my story about discovering joy in the journey. My prayer is that these words would resonate with you and you would be able to find joy and empowerment in your own story. I was reminded of how Jesus spoke through parables. He provided depth and colour to his teachings. I believe the reason he did this was to touch hearts in a way that is more powerful than anything else. This is my hope – to connect with you at a heart level.

If you had told me a year ago that I would be writing my story and sharing it with the world, I would have told you that I didn't have a story to share. I thought that something miraculous needed to happen in order to have something to share. I am realising that something miraculous has happened to me – I was created. Period.

This means that the same is true for YOU.

You were created.

You are a miracle.

Let me say that again – YOU are a miracle.

The chance of you being born, at this exact moment in time, is a miracle. You have something to offer to this world and that something is who you are – in ALL that this entails.

Most of my life I have been afraid to truly be seen. I've lived with shame and fear that if someone knew the true Jess that they would look at me differently. I have spent the past year peeling back the layers and identifying the different lenses that I have viewed my life through.

I have leaned into the fear of being seen by placing myself in communities where I am surrounded by amazing human beings who are simply a little further along on their journey than I am. In these spaces I have shared my heart and my desires, my dreams and my hopes. I have celebrated my wins and shared my fears and struggles with these women. So much healing has taken place.

Being in these communities of amazing women has brought up comparison. I would observe their life and see all of the wonderful qualities, and think "look at all that they have to offer." I would compare their amazing qualities to all of my shortfalls. What I am discovering is the importance of honouring everyone's strengths. When we are faced with comparison, it is so important to be gentle with ourselves and flip the script that is playing in our minds. Instead, look for ways we are similar to the person we admire and speak those qualities over ourselves.

One of the most impactful things that I have learned in these communities is being able to identify limiting beliefs, release them and replace them with truth. What we focus our attention on, expands. You may have noticed this when you were buying a new (to you) vehicle. They seem to appear everywhere! The same concept applies to our thoughts about ourselves. When I come across a belief that doesn't sit well with me I pause and ask is there truth to this statement? If not, I ask what is true? If we focus our thoughts and energies on what we lack, this will be reinforced. However, when we consciously choose to focus on who we truly are – it shifts EVERYTHING.

Ever since I can remember, I have associated my worth and identity with what I DO. Being able to embrace the fact that my worth is not defined by another human has been liberating. I have realised that it isn't about having the right words or the perfect credentials, but simply turning to God and knowing that he has created me and that is enough.

I feel that it is important to take a moment and recognize that we are all at different points along our journey. I had a sweet moment this week with my counsellor. I have been working with her for a year and she wanted to take a moment and review why I started working with her. My original goal was to gain tangible ways to help "get through the day." It came from a place of "I can't do this, help me, save me." What I desire to express to you, is that this is OK. It is ok to be in that space. Awareness and seeking support are the first steps. I truly didn't believe that I had the strength to do it. If you are at the place in your life where you are in survival mode (like I was, and sometimes still feel like I am) and find it difficult to step into your true power, I want you to know that I see you, I know you, I am you.

I am so thankful that she took a moment to pause and reflect on the past year and the amount of growth that I have experienced. It is a daily choice to remember that I have the power within me to face any circumstance. The more that I look back, remember and show my brain the proof of how I have come through whatever situation has presented itself, the more gratitude wells up within me. I am reminded that I have been supported and will continue to be supported.

Visualisation Exercise:

I want to take a moment to do an exercise to tap into your own intuition and power. I was fortunate to be on the receiving end of this visualisation and it had such an impact on me that I wanted to create space for you to experience it as well.

Take a deep breath and pause. In your mind, picture your 5 year-old self. What is she doing? Where is she? Imagine her pause and see you walking up to her. She greets you with the biggest smile and the warmest hug. She has something to say. Lean in for a moment. Ask "what would you like to say to me?" Take all the time right now to listen to her – there is no rush, you have all the time in the world. Take a moment to write what she desires you to know.

Now give your 5 year old self a huge hug. Thank her for this moment.

Now, I want you to ask your 5 year old self "is there anything that you want to know?"

Write down what you want to tell your 5 year-old self?

You give your 5 year old self a huge hug and thank her. You wave to her and come back to the present moment.

Take another deep breath, maybe place your hand on your heart. Now let's imagine your future self. You walk down a path that leads you to her. What is your 70-year-old self you doing? Where is she? What does 70 year old you want you to know? I encourage you to write it.

Take another breath and thank her for their words. You wave to her as you walk back down the path to your current self. Give yourself a huge hug and take a sip of water.

Was there anything that you were surprised about? I want to encourage you to share your experience with someone that you trust. When we speak about our experiences, I have found that they have a stronger impact on our subconscious.

In honour of my request to speak, I want to share my experience. My 5 year old self said to me "where have you been? I've been waiting on you (to play)." I wanted my 5 year old self to know how precious she is, and to hold onto the sparkle that she had. My 70 year old self was at a cottage, watering plants on the front porch and her eyes lit up when she saw me coming. She embraced me with such a warm, strong hug. She told me how proud of me she was. How she saw my strength in my darkest moments.

It would be an honour to hear your experience with this exercise. I would love it if you shared it with me!

I want to encourage you to pause and place a reminder on your calendar one year from today. My hope is that you carve out time to reflect on all the growth that you have experienced. Anchor into this – Journal it. See how fabulous you truly are.

I am a huge Harry Potter fan and as I have been pondering about my purpose, the image of a phoenix came to me. It reminded me to see the beauty in the ashes, for out of the ashes we rise. I am claiming this for myself and for you. The release of that which is no longer serving you with the promise of the birth of something greater. When we actively choose to face our fears and experience life as an opportunity to learn, grow and expand, we see the difficult moments with a different perspective. Trusting that when we release, it will transform into something greater.

I am claiming my purpose – I am a legacy of light, here to bring awareness to the truth of who we are. To point you towards the things that can breathe life into your lungs. As I shine my light, you are awakened, ignited, and moved to do the same. I invite you to hop into your hot air balloon and go far and wide. To find the joy in your journey, to be the phoenix that rises from the ashes. And in doing so, I think you'll find how amazing it is.

And this is how it all begins…

BIO:

Jessica Jarels is an aspiring entrepreneur on a mission to help women discover joy in their journey.

www.instagram.com/discovering.joy.in.the.journey

24
WHY THE WORLD NEEDS MORE FEMALE LEADERS

Elena Daccus

I woke up in the middle of the night on one particularly hot summer's day filled with absolute joy, hope and happiness inside. I saw an amazing dream, where I saw our world filled with businesses run by women, female CEOs, founders, presidents, prime ministers from all backgrounds, religions and races. The world where we never have to discuss diversity, it is not even a point of conversation as it is an absolute norm. A world where there are no wars, no borders, but there is freedom, collaboration and where everyone is accepted for who they are.

This is the world I am on the mission to help create, this a mission that fires my soul so deeply inside.

You see, when I was ten years old growing up in communist Soviet Union, I was never told that you could do anything, you can be anything and that the world is full of possibility.

In fact it was quite the opposite, I grew up with all the

mindset issues and limiting beliefs that you can imagine. In fact, when I was ten years old a teacher asked us to write an essay to tell "Who do you want to be when you grow up?". I was so excited, so hopefully when my mind started thinking about this, I started wondering who do I want to be? My mind went in all the places and I wrote a deep, heartfelt essay about how the world needs more female leaders and I wanted to be one of them.

I will never forget that day, when I was so nervous and excited to share my ambitious goals with my teacher, she read it in front of the whole class, looked at and laughed out loud, paused and said in front of all the whole class "The best thing you can be Elena, the best thing you can be is a secretary of the local factory! These big dreams are not for you!"

Boom. Crash. I felt like a large brick just hit my head. I still remember that feeling so vividly, when someone so abruptly puts a huge heavy cap on your dreams. I was so hurt, so full of shame, so embarrassed.

Fast forward twenty years later and I am sitting in one of the most glamorous offices in London. My secretary just brought me my cup of coffee and papers for the upcoming board meeting. I sat across one of the worlds largest boardroom tables, leading negotiations of a multi-billion dollar deal. I am the youngest and only female across the boardroom table, looking around I could not be more grateful and could not be more proud of what I have achieved, I have bought and sold over 50 companies worth over $10bn, opened the lids to hundreds of businesses, supported world's best founders and CEOs. I thought to myself, how different my life could have turned out if I believed my teacher.

This is why I love supporting women, helping female entrepreneurs, experts, coaches consultants, create outstanding businesses, as behind every woman, there is a positive impact on the world. Every time a woman succeeds, she sets an example of what is possible. I want to help her go beyond her wildest dreams, achieve what naysayers said would never work and is impossible. So that the next time someone puts a cap on a child's dreams and tells them it is impossible and their dreams are limited, our kids can say... " That is not true! Look at my mom, she did it!".

I want this story of success to be yours too, yes for you reading this right now. I know you are searching for something more, for more impact, more meaning. You are probably looking around your life and on the surface you are a picture of success, but you are feeling numb inside and wondering if this is it, if this all your life is about. You have a fire, a deep drive to be more, show more, create legacy, create impact with your work, with your words and with your business.

The truth is I was there, feeling exactly the same. It was after my first son was born and it was a particularly heavy work period. I am in the office at 7am and stay in the office till 9pm, I have missed every single bedtime and have not seen my baby for 6 days.

I felt so numb, so broken inside. I remember sitting in this cold toilet cubicle pumping breast milk, two devices attached to my breasts. Tears are streaming down my cheeks. I remember thinking what is the point of this? Is this all my life will be? If I died tomorrow, did my life really matter?

In that moment, I thought I want to work, I want to help women, I want to create legacy and I also want to be with my kids. This was the moment when my search for freedom creating systems began.

I got completely obsessed with finding the way not just to create wealth and impact, but also freedom so that mothers can run powerful, successful businesses, create generational wealth for their family and have time freedom and complete control over their destiny.

One of the most amazing aspects of mergers and acquisitions is you get to see how business really operates, you get to see and understand the whole sector. What works and what does not, what sells and what does not. Why one company on the surface of it looks amazing, lots of followers, celebrity status, but inside the founder is trapped within it, can't sell it, can't scale, hating their clients and business model, desperately trying to exit, but can't as business is worth nothing without its founder.

Through this quest I discovered what successful companies had in common and what failed businesses missed to implement, which I have put into my signature framework Power-House CEO - which I now teach to expert based businesses in the online space.

It is during that time that I met Emily. I remember the first day opening the lid to her business. I was amazed, low cost of customer acquisition, clients stayed with her for life and customer value was through the roof. I remember trying to book a meeting with her and I called her secretary who said: "Well it will be difficult, as Emily works from 10am to 3pm as she has four children and does all the pick-ups and drop off herself!". My mind was blown, I wanted to scream inside: "Wow I found it, I found the way to to create huge impact and wealth and also freedom to be with my kids!".

What Emily did was so simple, it absolutely blew my mind. She had just one powerful highly converting presentation, that every time she shared that presentation at least 20% of the audience said yes to buying from her. The most amazing thing is, this presentation is completely pitch free, it is authentic, rooted in your story and without any icky sales tactics everyone else teaches. All that Emily did was change her audience and used the power of other people's virtual stages to grow.

You see most people when they start their expert online business, they do it in a wrong way. They have acquired so much knowledge, so much expertise, they experienced a personal transformation and want to share it with other people.

Just like one of my clients Catherine did. She came across my podcast and knew she wanted to work with me. She helped mothers to stop generational cycles of trauma. She had a traumatic childhood and went on a journey to become a better parent. She read all the books, took all the courses, spent years learning the key transformational tools to become a better parent and now helped her clients to achieve the same. Like everyone else she created an Instagram, Facebook account and started posting online and provided so much information, tutorials, valuable content, as that is exactly what marketing gurus tell you to do.

She worked so hard, in fact she worked more and saw her kids less when she had in her 9-5 job. She was providing so much information and that information itself could have changed people's life, but no-one seemed to care, no one was asking to buy from her. She got some sales one month and felt so excited, but then nothing, crickets, no sales. Business felt like a complete emotional rollercoaster, she did not know where the next client will be coming from. Sales were inconsistent and cashflow was unreliable. She felt so frustrated looking at people around her, who were half as good as her and so less qualified than her, but making way more money than her and she could not understand why.

The problem was Catherine was making the same mistake most people make in this business, they try to sell with information. You hear this from marketing gurus all the time, just provide value and clients will come. Well you have been doing that, but clients are not coming.

You see this strategy worked 3 years ago when online business was way less saturated, 3 years ago starting an online business was like opening the only food shop in town. When you are the only food shop in town you don't need to be the best or have the best strategy. It does not work anymore when there are hundreds of shops in town, when anyone can create content for free and they don't even need to be an expert.

What Emily did and what I teach all my clients is a different strategy, is it the true freedom creating system. First you need to create your own lane, your unique positioning, create powerful messaging, craft a powerful presentation that when people hear you speak they want to work with you. Then you need to use virtual stages to amplify your message. Virtual stages are amazing, as you don't have to travel and people have already collected an audience of perfect clients for you, so you don't have to wait years building your own following before you start creating consistent high ticket sales in your business.

This is how parenting coach Catherine went from feeling like an invisible unheard expert to now signing consistently 1-3 high ticket clients every single week and making multiple 5 figures each month. In fact all my clients sign 20% of the audience every time they speak, like my client Elisabeth who signed 6 high ticket clients after one podcast interview or my client Jessica signing 10 clients after this one presentation during the Virtual Summit.

This is how you create a consistent reliable cash generation system in your business.

This is how you create stable cashflow and you need stable cashflow to grow, to scale, to impact more people. I know your work can change people's lives, your business needs to be seen by people.

There is a reason you are feeling this calling inside, that drive inside your soul. You were called to create this incredible business. You are meant to impact the world with your mission, you are meant to be the wealthiest of your family and friends. So that everyone who ever doubted you, who called you crazy for starting this journey, soon will be asking " How did you do it?"

BIO:

Elena Daccus is a High Ticket Sales Expert. She went from a girl full of limiting beliefs, who was told the best thing she can be is work as the secretary at the local factory to the youngest and the only female across the world's largest boardroom tables. She is the goto expert when it comes to messaging and high ticket sales. She will show you how to drastically simplify your business, stop 90% of stuff that is keeping you stuck and skyrocket your business with one powerful message and virtual stages.

www.instagram.com/bossyheelsclub

25
AN UNEXPECTED JOURNEY

Jess Sansom

I launched Sansom VA in October 2019 after 17 years of working as a full-time primary school teacher. During that time, I had many roles - teacher, mentor, line manager, subject leader, SENCo, Acting Assistant Headteacher to name but a few! All of which had vast amounts of admin, policies and red tape! I became a whizz at multitasking, working to deadlines, talking to outside agencies and stakeholders and chairing many, many meetings. I also drank a lot of tea!

But when the time came for me to have my own family my dreams quickly changed to becoming my own leader. I wanted to create a work-life balance that meant I could spend more time with my family and be free to go to school assemblies and school trips with my children when they came up.

I love what I do now because of the creativity it gives me, the connections I make with people and most of all the freedom it gives me to be flexible around my kids ... but it wasn't always this way!

Flashback 6 years and I was battling (and it really did feel like a war inside and out) to cope with a teaching career and a nearly 5-year-old about to start school. I had a moment in the school car park where I realised, I just didn't want to be there anymore. I sobbed, fighting the urge to start the car and just drive away. I hated that I was spending more time with other people's kids than my own. I wasn't doing either job, teacher or mother, well. Something had to change.

That day I handed in my notice. I had no job and no plan, gulp!

The sense of relief was massive but the crushing guilt about putting my family at financial risk was almost overwhelming. I very nearly went in and asked for my job back. But the universe has a way of giving you a sign to let you know you are on the right path. Due to the stress of the job, I had struggled to fall pregnant with my first child. Heartbreakingly though, we had been trying for over four years for my second and we had just about given up. However, one month after handing my notice in I fell pregnant with my second. So, I knew it was just meant to be!

A year went by, and I knew I needed to go back to work after my maternity leave, but I just could not face going back to a career that didn't value me or my family life. Teaching is the most rewarding job you can do. Yes, giving them an education is important but watching them grow and develop into caring, happy, decent little humans made my heart sing every day. That's what made it so hard to walk away but I knew I had to.

But what could I do next?

I felt trapped ... until I met another very smiley mum on the school playground at pick-up time. We were both excited and nervous to see how our little ones had spent their first day at big school, so to pass the time the mummy small talk started!!

Over the coming weeks a friendship grew, and the subject of jobs came up. I explained my situation and then the pivotal moment happened!

She said, "Have you thought about being a VA? You have loads of transferable skills especially with your background in education and running your own classroom."

Fireworks went off in my head! I had suddenly found my place in the world again, hooray.

Then the questions started ... where do I start? I had never heard of a VA before, never mind knowing if I could be one. And running my own business, could I really do that? From an early age I, like most kids of my generation, was told the path was school – university – job. The idea that I could go out and do something different and people pay me on my terms had never even entered my head before. Being an entrepreneur was something other people did, wasn't it?

I was so uplifted and excited by discovering a whole new world that my mind suddenly became a sponge! I wanted to learn everything, and boy was there a lot to learn. I googled all these different inspiring women that mentored VA's, read every article and blog I could find about working remotely and running your own business, I had to learn business finances, insurance, GDPR, marketing ... the list went on! It has been such an incredible whirlwind journey learning all the things that go into creating a business but learning all the things just made me want to be a VA even more.

I very quickly fell into a role as a general VA for a CEO of a charity managing her inbox and appointment diary. It snowballed into helping other members of staff at the charity managing more inboxes, organising events, managing social media among other things. All was going swimmingly for three months ... and then the pandemic hit, and the charity couldn't afford to pay me anymore.

Like so many around the country I found myself stuck at

home with a toddler, home-schooling another and very little brain space to take on finding clients. But my training kicked in, I found my strength. I knew as a women/teacher/mother I can do anything because we do everything, right!

I gave myself space to really think about what I wanted to do as a business, which VA tasks actually brought me joy, because if we don't love what we do what is the point. I spent time in Facebook business groups and networking, getting to know the small business community and letting them get to know me. Someone once said to me 'it's not about catching someone at the perfect time in a Facebook group and shouting about your services, although that sometimes happens, it's more about showing up so that when their perfect time comes up its your name that they think about.

I had noticed a common thread in all these groups, the top task that is hated or is mentioned when considering outsourcing was social media. Well, this was actually something I enjoyed doing (strange I know!). I get a thrill from playing around with beautiful colours, shapes and pictures, and finally putting my degree in art history to some use! I loved creating eye-catching graphics that were on brand, adding short and snappy captions that have purpose and seeing how proud people felt when their platforms grew and looked professional.

I knew I could build a service where I could help small business owners with their social media planning, creating and scheduling, all in one package, helping them to have confidence with their visibility and making their products or services stand out from the crowd. I had found my niche!

I re-launched myself as a Social Media VA in April 2021. And at the time of writing this it will be my 1st business birthday tomorrow. My mind is blown if I think back and appreciate everything I have achieved and how much I have learnt over the last year.

I would love to say it all went smoothly but as with everything it has been a bumpy journey. I didn't get my first client for 6 weeks which was extremely nerve wracking. It made me question my choices again. But I persevered and I have never looked back.

The day I got my very first client was amazing. Not just because I finally had income coming in, which to be honest was a massive relief, but because I felt proud of myself. It was a feeling I hadn't had for a long, long time. I had created something for myself, and it had worked. I literally gave the lovely lady (who knows who she is!) a huge hug, she was a bit shocked to say the least. But I was so grateful that she believed in me to do a good job, it made me believe in me too.

I now spend my days working with amazing women that are brave and strong and run phenomenal businesses. Their tenacity to keep learning and growing is what spurs me on to continue building my business. I know social media isn't everyone's cup of tea, so if I can give the gift of time to just a few people by taking a draining but necessary task away and make sure they have time for their families instead I feel I have won.

I never expected to be running my own business, I thought I would be teaching forever. It's funny how the universe has its own, sometimes unexpected, ideas.

BIO:

Jess is a Social Media VA whose goal is to help small business owners achieve a sense of relief that their social media is done!

Jess aims to give people an established presence online by posting consistently, planning content so it is balanced, and making business services or products stand out and sparkle – all done for you!

Jess has a wealth of experience from working with wedding

photographers, beauticians, HR companies, restaurant owners, Celebrants, business coaches and much more.

If you're thinking, it's time to get online but you need a bit of help, get in touch.

www.sansomva.co.uk

ABOUT THE DAISY CHAIN GROUP

Trudy Simmons started The Daisy Chain Group in 2010. It was started to support and encourage businesswomen to have a safe space to share their journeys, to grow their businesses and to be seen and heard in their endeavours.

Since its inception, the concept has grown to include platforms for women to find their voice and become more visible in lots of different ways. Whether it is attending online networking events, committing to co-working time together, learning from experts in masterclasses or investing in monthly business coaching to boost your clarity, direction, focus, accountability and momentum, we all need to find the space to work ON our businesses.

If you have a story to share, come and be a part of the Shine On You Crazy Daisy book series and share your story, or be on the Shine On You Crazy Daisy Podcast to give your story gravitas and hear it in your own voice.

Trudy is known for her engaged communities on Facebook – Businesswomen Shine Online and The Hampshire Women's Business Group

HAVING FUN in your business is a core value of The Daisy

Chain Group. Having fun and TAKING ACTION is what builds you AND your business.

You can find The Daisy Chain Group here:
    https://www.thedaisychaingroup.com
    https://www.facebook.com/daisychaingroup
    https://www.instagram.com/daisychaingroup/
    https://www.linkedin.com/in/trudysimmons/

You can find The Daisy Chain Group communities here:
    https://www.facebook.com/
groups/businesswomenshineonline
    https://www.facebook.com/
groups/hampshirewomensbusiness

You can find our services here:
    Shine On You Crazy Daisy Membership - https://www.
thedaisychaingroup.com/shine-on-you-crazy-daisy-
membership
    You can listen to the Shine On You Crazy Daisy Podcast here:
    https://www.thedaisychaingroup.com/podcasts/shine-on-you-crazy-daisy

EVERY TIME YOU BUY FROM A SMALL BUSINESS, THEY DO A HAPPY DANCE!

PLEASE SUPPORT THE BUSINESSES IN THIS BOOK.

CHARITY LINK

10% of the profits from this book will be donated to Healthcare Workers' Foundation Family Fund. The fund will support the children and families of healthcare workers who have passed due to Covid-19. To donate or support this incredible charity, please go to this link

www.healthcareworkersfoundation.org

OTHER BOOKS

AVAILABLE NOW

Shine On You Crazy Daisy – Volume 1
Shine On You Crazy Daisy – Volume 2
Shine On You Crazy Daisy – Volume 3
Shine On You Crazy Daisy – Volume 4

Available on Amazon, iBook and in all good bookshops.

COMING SOON

Shine On You Crazy Daisy – Volume 6

Available in Summer 2022 – more stories, more inspiration, more motivation to get out there and do what you WANT to do with your business.

We are all in this together.

Shine On...

Printed in Great Britain
by Amazon